YOU ARE
AWESOME

For Evie and Teddy. You are awesome!

Published by Sourcebooks eXplore, an imprint of Sourcebooks Kids.
P.O. Box 4410, Naperville, Illinois 60567-4410
(630) 961-3900
sourcebookskids.com

Originally published in 2018 in Great Britain by Wren & Rook, an imprint
of Hachette Children's Group, part of Hodder and Stoughton.

Library of Congress Cataloging-in-Publication Data is on file with the publisher.

Source of Production: 1010 Printing International, Kwun Tong, Hong Kong, China
Date of Production: March 2022
Run Number: 5025642

Printed and bound in China.
OGP 10 9 8 7 6 5

YOU ARE AWESOME

Matthew Syed

ILLUSTRATED BY

TOBY TRIUMPH

sourcebooks
eXplore

CONTENTS

Getting good at stuff is not as hard as you might think. In fact, anyone can get (much) better at almost anything.

BUT YOU'RE BUSY, RIGHT?

Tell me about it. There's so much to do—sports, hobbies, time with friends, keeping up with homework… Finding the time to **do** everything can be a challenge. Trying to be **good** at everything can be even harder.

That's where this book comes in. It's going to let you into the secret to being awesome, and tell you things that people at the top of their game know about success. If you've got a friend who seems to ace exams with no effort, or a brother who is annoyingly better than you at tennis, or even if you just feel like you're not quite sure what you're best at—then this book is for you.

What's involved? Well, we're going to get up close and personal with success, delve inside our brains to understand how we learn new skills, and equip you with strategies to build your confidence and fulfill your potential. We'll bust some myths along the way about what it takes to stand out from the crowd, share some stories of how super-successful people made it to the top, and provide all the support and advice you need to achieve your personal awesomeness.

So, if you're up for the challenge then let's get started… We haven't got any time to waste if you want to be an awesome vlogger, pianist, physicist, tennis pro, chess champion, deep sea diver, heart surgeon, president, computer hacker, CIA agent, soccer player, mathematician, archaeologist, teacher, plumber, attorney, judge, chef, travel writer, dog groomer, TV presenter, basketball player, rock star, astronaut, or cheese sprayer (no, me neither on that last one, but apparently it is a thing, and if you're going to be one, you might as well be awesome at it).

Oh, and by the way, those people with that perfect selfie, that great math test score, or the amazing piano performance? They were lying if they said they didn't practice…

1.

*Imagine a very ordinary kid. Living on a completely ordinary street. On the outskirts of a totally ordinary town. You can probably see where we're going with this already. This kid (let's call him **Kid A**) probably spends his weekends hanging out in the ordinary shopping mall, and then goes home to eat an ordinary dinner in his ordinary house. Yep, you've got it. It's all fairly, um, ordinary…*

As for the town's famous sons and daughters—you know, people born in the area who went on to do great things and change the world—well, there really aren't many. Apart from a TV weatherman and a guy who might—no one is quite sure—have invented a crucial bit of the tumble dryer in the 1980s. But that's it. Honestly, this place is duller than a dull day in **Dullsville.**

So, I hear you asking, why are we beginning this book here? What's the point of zoning in on **Kid A**, in his ordinary bunk bed in his ordinary bedroom? Well, that's exactly the point—**Kid A** IS ordinary. Just like any other kid. Perhaps just like you? But something amazing is about to happen.

KID A'S LIFE IS ABOUT TO CHANGE. FOREVER.

Now, he isn't going to be bitten by a radioactive spider or struck by a thunderbolt that gives him...

Instead, returning from school one day, **Kid A**'s mom and dad are outside the house waiting for him.

They are up to something. **Kid A** is sure of it. His mom is hopping backward and forward like an overexcited frog and his dad is smiling. Yes, smiling. And **Kid A** knows that this can only mean one thing. They've got some kind of surprise in store.

"Close your eyes," squeals his mom mid-leap.
Kid A complies, but inside he is seriously hoping this doesn't turn out to be anything like the last "surprise" they pulled. The one with the trampoline, which ended with an embarrassing call to the fire department...
With great excitement, Dad hauls open the garage door. "Right, you can look now!"

For a moment, **Kid A** thinks he's missing something. His parents stand beside him, beaming with pride.

"Um, it's a table," says **Kid A**, sounding puzzled.

"I know it looks like an old table," says his dad, springing forward, "but SEE, it's a table-tennis table!"

Before **Kid A** can respond, his mom thrusts a table-tennis racket and ball into his hand, and before he can say "ping-pong paddle," he's facing his dad across the net.

"What are you waiting for?" his mom shrieks, now close to a mild frenzy. His dad is also looking positively dangerous. Like he might injure himself or someone else in the close vicinity. He's doing wild warm-up stretches with his legs and bending into positions that **Kid A** has never seen before (except maybe the ones you might see in a pretzel).

"Come on, let's have a go!" his dad shouts from the other side of the table.

Kid A stares over the net at his dad. His evening really has taken an unexpected turn. But in spite of this, he holds the racket ready and waits for his dad to serve… and this is where we press the pause button on the story. Why? Because **Kid A** has reached a big fork in his life.

NO, NOT THAT
KIND OF FORK!

The kind where he faces a choice between two paths. One path will see him carry on living his ordinary, unremarkable life. The other path will take him on an **awesome and incredible journey**, and it all comes down to what happens next.

3

But let's save the best for last, and begin with the path that leads to **Kid A** becoming…

KID AVERAGE

OK, back to the story. Concentrating hard, **Kid Average** waits (slightly longer than he thought he might have to. His dad went back into the house to get his lucky sports headband). Next thing he knows, the ball comes whizzing across the net like a bullet. And **Kid Average** misses it. Completely. Well, that was unlucky, he thinks. Dad seems good at this. Maybe he just got lucky though. Or maybe it was those stretches (or that headband). **Kid Average** tries again. This time, the ball slices sideways, bounces off the table, and spins out of the garage door.

"Never mind," says his dad. "Try again."
Turning a fancy shade of beetroot, **Kid Average** is not exactly enjoying this.

He makes another attempt at serving. This time, the ball scrapes over the net, only for his father to return the serve with such force that the ball comes back at him like a missile. It connects with his end of the table and then hits him full force on the elbow.

"Come on, buddy!" shouts his dad, still jumping around like a pro. "You can do better than that."

Kid Average collects the ball from the garage floor and considers asking for the headband to use as a bandage. He shuffles back to the table but his heart just isn't in it. As far as he's concerned, he could face further humiliation from his dad (who seems to have found his inner Olympian) or be in his bedroom with his video game console. Just then, the console wins.

"I've had enough," he says, setting the racket on the table. "But thanks anyway."

For a while, his parents blame each other. Or rather his mom blames his dad for being too competitive, but it quickly becomes clear that **Kid Average** just doesn't have the **fire** in him to take up the challenge.

"But I'm no good at it," protests **Kid Average** when his dad suggests a game the following week. And, to be fair, his bruises have only just faded from the last time...

"Why don't you practice with Andrew?" his mom suggests. This is **Kid Average**'s worst nightmare. Never mind his dad, his brother is more competitive than LeBron James in the playoffs. There is no way he wants he wants to play against that guy, who is bound to tell everyone at school about it too.

"No thanks," sighs **Kid Average**, who goes to his bedroom. "He's bound to be better than me anyway."

Time goes by. His dad takes up golf, and the table-tennis table in the garage begins to gather dust. His mom piles his dad's new golf clubs on it for a while, before she gets fed up with the lack of space. Eventually she takes it apart, stacks it to one side, and sells it to their next-door neighbor for an absolute bargain.

Meanwhile, **Kid Average** continues to shuffle through life. His school reports suggest he could try harder, but it never happens. In his eyes, challenges are obstacles, and definitely best avoided. Instead, he ignores his parents' pleas to get out more and rarely leaves his room. There, with his console in hand and snacks within easy reach, he sets about, well… doing…

It's fair to say that **Kid Average** is living up to his name.

But one day he's flipping through sports channels, looking for something to pass the time, when he comes across a live stream of the National Table Tennis Championship Finals. Seeing this brings his not-so-amazing ping-pong debut back to him. The match is taking place inside a huge hall, watched by hundreds of spectators. The camera zooms in on the player with the ball in hand. He's totally focused and completely calm, as if perhaps he's been working toward this moment for a long time. **Kid Average** sits up straight. His attention is glued to the screen. Because the player on the screen in front of him, preparing to serve for the championship, looks strikingly familiar…

KID AWESOME

Now let's rewind to the point where **Kid A**'s story reached that fork in the path. He's facing his dad across the net, remember? **Kid A**'s first attempt at hitting the ball goes seriously badly wrong. The second try is worse and the third attempt results in a bruise the size of the table-tennis ball on his elbow. Unlike **Kid Average**, however, he doesn't give up.

Instead he feels some kind of knot in his stomach. At first, he thinks it might be the two chocolate bars he had at recess. But that's not it. It's something else. He realizes that he wants to put up a fight, to get a bit better, and to show his dad that he can win at least one point off him.

OK, so he knows he's got some improving to do. Actually, that is the understatement of the millennium. He has got absolutely stacks of improving to do, but instead of putting down the racket and burying his head back into his laptop, he tells himself that, if he tries, in time he might just do a bit better. After all, what's the worst that could happen? And at the very least, his mom might dial down the excitable frog moves. So, rather than quitting right there and right then, he picks up the ball and tries again.

And again, And again, And again...

(OK, so you get the point…)
An hour later, he's yet to score a point against his dad. But he's quite a lot better, there have been no further ping-pong–induced injuries, and he's learning from the experience. Every now and then, he even

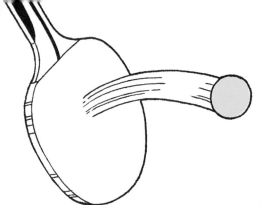

surprises himself with a half-decent return serve, and there was a moment when he almost put a shot past his dad…

Now admittedly, **Kid A** is not going to win any prizes (yet), but he's making minor improvements and is definitely a little bit better than totally useless. And what's more, he's quite enjoying it. It turns out that this surprise was one of his parents' better ideas.

While **Kid Average** has decided he's no good, given up completely, and gone to bed, **Kid Awesome** is determined and sticks to it. He **really** wants to improve. Not just by a little bit, but as far as he can take things. **Kid Awesome** is set on becoming the best table-tennis player he can, and he realizes that this all comes down to how often he can get in the garage to practice. He starts to love the game. So much so that he has even started thinking about asking his brother to help him practice.

Strangely, **Kid Awesome** has stopped minding that his brother might be better than him. Well, that's not quite true. He minds (a bit) less. Because the fact that his brother is better forces **Kid Awesome** to work even harder at the game. Together, the pair put in so many hours at the table that their dad has to check on them to make sure that everyone is still in one piece. But thanks to spending so much time with a racket in hand, **Kid Awesome** starts to learn from his mistakes, and picks up skills that no amount of stretching from his dad or brother could ever hope to match.

Word spreads through the street that table tennis is pretty good fun. And what happens in an ordinary town, when someone gets something new? Yep, you guessed it. Everyone wants one. Before **Kid Awesome** knows it, the whole area is **wild for ping-pong**. The table-tennis club at school is inundated with new members.

By now, with plenty of practice (after school, most weekends and holidays), **Kid Awesome** is beyond good. He joins a regional team on a winning streak and then, to the delight of his parents (their table-tennis table purchase now seeming like a twenty-four-karat gold idea), his brother, and everyone who has played a role in this long journey, he makes it to the final of the National Championships…

The match is streamed live. **Kid Awesome** finds himself under the spotlights and under pressure, but he's ready for this moment. He's been training hard, and all his preparations are going to plan. It's a tough match, his greatest challenge yet. **Kid Awesome's** opponent proves to be skilful and a bit cunning, but he doesn't lose his cool. He battles hard and finds himself at match point. All of a sudden, with the audience holding their breath, he realizes just how far he's come. For years now, he's been getting up early to practice, and loving the challenge of improving his game. With this in mind, he serves for the match and…

WINS!

And that's the thing about dreams—they can come true. But unlike all those fairy tales we hear about, they don't happen by accident.

That's where the book in your hands comes in. It's all about how we turn our dreams into something we really can achieve.

Now, we're not talking about those fantasy type of dreams where your school is invaded during a zombie apocalypse. We aren't even talking about major dreams—you know, the one where you're receiving an **Oscar** for directing a Hollywood blockbuster or you've been awarded the **Nobel Peace Prize** for your services to international diplomacy.

NO, WE'RE TALKING ABOUT THE DREAMS YOU HAVE OF LANDING THAT PART IN THE SCHOOL PLAY, OF (FINALLY) MAKING THE SPORTS TEAM, OF HITTING ALL THE RIGHT NOTES IN CHOIR PRACTICE, OR EVEN IMPROVING SIGNIFICANTLY ON THE NEXT MATH TEST.

Whatever your ambition, even if it seems out of your reach right now, this book is all about how to fulfill your potential and achieve it. This might seem like a bold promise, but there's one more thing you need to know about **Kid Awesome**. That boy who chose the path to becoming a champion?

IT WAS ME.

My name is Matthew. Some years ago, I became the British number one table-tennis player. I even represented Great Britain in the Olympics, which is worthy of a fist bump, right? Now, it would be very easy for me to pretend this was down to a natural talent. I could boast that I was born with lightning-quick reactions, but that would be a fib. Yes, when I won the crown I had a reputation for speed, gutsiness, and quick wits, but I cannot honestly say that I arrived in this world with a ping-pong racket in my hand. My background is as unremarkable as I described. I was very average. An OK kid, but with nothing to hint that I could become an elite athlete. Nothing to suggest that I could be **AWESOME**.

The truth is I had to learn the skills I needed to become the best. Not only that, I had to start from scratch. Yes, my parents were table-tennis fans, which gave me a small head start over my friends, but I had to practice with passion and dedication to learn my skills. It was hard work, with a lot of setbacks on the way, but I gained valuable lessons from every moment.

So, let's forget those types of stories that we hear about people being "born gifted" or "naturally talented" when it comes to explaining how someone got really good at something. I'm here to reveal the truth, and the fact that it's possible for anyone to get really good at (almost) anything—and that includes **YOU**.

So, let's break down the factors that earned me the crown as the table-tennis prince. And I'm warning you now, it's all about grit, not glamour…

1 THE TABLE

My parents are still unable to explain why they decided to fill their garage with a full-size table-tennis table—a super-deluxe model with gold lettering, since you ask. Even so, I can be sure there weren't many kids that had one, which gave me a head start. It didn't make me instantly better than anyone else, though; I simply started practicing earlier than most. As time went by, people began to say I was "a genius with the racket" and that I had a "**natural talent**." But they hadn't seen the table in my garage. And they definitely hadn't seen how many rainy Sundays and evenings after school I'd spent in there, tirelessly batting the ball back and forth in an effort to improve.

It makes you think, doesn't it? Is there someone awesome that you think is just naturally brilliant at something? I wonder what they've got in their garage…?

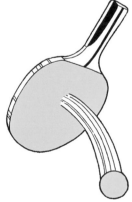

2 MY OLDER BROTHER

My brother is awesome. And luckily he is also hugely competitive.
True story—he used to make me play pool with three balls missing
from the table. That way, if I beat him, he could tell his friends that he
hadn't really lost. He maintained it wasn't an actual match if some of
the balls were missing. Crazy times.

But it wasn't just snooker—he wanted to be the best at table tennis
too. And he was awesome (did I mention that?). So, he became my
"ready to go at any moment" kind of practice partner. He was as
available as a **twenty-four-hour McDonald's**, so with a table in the
garage we would duel before school, and spend hours in the evenings
whipping the ball back and forth. I can't lie, I secretly wanted to
dominate each match and leave my brother begging for mercy, and
I've no doubt he wanted to do the same to me. So, we battled it out
together, testing each other's reflexes and experimenting with new
moves. Without realizing it, he and I put in thousands of hours of
practice, and it showed in our razor-sharp skills.

3 A TEACHER WITH A PASSION FOR PING-PONG!

Chances are you can name a teacher who loves their subject. When
they're all fired up about sharing their knowledge, or know how to
make you laugh as you learn, their enthusiasm is infectious, and
before you know it, you're enjoying it as much as they are.

At school, Mr. Charters was a good teacher, but it was his passion for sports that had the biggest impact on me. He had bright eyes, a black beard, and a wonderful way of encouraging you to give it your all.

"**Life is about being the best you can possibly be**," he said. While he ran almost all of the after-school clubs, it was table tennis that meant the most to him. He also happened to be one of the nation's top coaches, and a talent scout on the lookout for players with potential to learn and improve. It meant that he encouraged anyone who showed the slightest interest in the sport to check out the local table-tennis club. Its name was Omega.

4 **THE LOCAL CLUB**

Imagine a super-exclusive center for the finest table-tennis players in the country… and then forget it. Despite having "mega" in its title, Omega was anything but. It was pretty much just a run-down hut with a couple of tables. It was very basic—freezing cold in the winter and sweltering in the summer, but a **magnet** for young players like me.

Once you had demonstrated that you knew a chop from a forehand slice (technical table-tennis shots rather than cuts of raw meat, in case you were concerned) you would be granted the ultimate honor: a key to Omega. This wasn't just any key, but one that opened the door day or night to the table-tennis palace (for "palace," read "shack") of my hometown.

I'd like to say that I had the honor of being the only keyholder, but in reality, most of the kids on the streets around mine also had one. As a result, the local area began to boast an unusually high number of young, **prizewinning** table-tennis players.

Now here's something to consider… When I played table tennis for England, many of the top players in the country (men and women) came from my street in Reading. Not the surrounding area, but my **ACTUAL STREET**. That is quite weird, don't you think? About as weird as the whole cast of Harry Potter being born in the same cul-de-sac in Chelmsford. Or is it? (They weren't by the way—the Harry Potter cast—I just made that up to illustrate my point.)

You see, it all comes down to how you become awesome at stuff. Which (remember) is what this book is all about. Lots of people seem to think that you need to be born with certain "gifts," or "talents." But if that is true, why were so many of the "**gifted**" and "**talented**" table-tennis players born on my ordinary street in Reading? It doesn't make any sense.

It only starts to make sense once you realize that it wasn't their "gifts" or "talents" that were making all these kids so much better at table tennis than the kids ten streets away. Instead, it was their access to Omega, to Mr. Charters, and all of the hours they spent practicing together. Quite simply, the kids ten streets away didn't do that.

Now, table tennis might not be your thing, and that's OK. We're all drawn to different interests and hobbies. At the same time, rest assured that this book isn't simply about getting **gold medals** or **excellent exam grades**. Oh no. Whether you want to master street magic, pull off awesome skateboard stunts, or bake the perfect cupcake, knowing that you don't have to be born "gifted" at these things to be good at them is really important. Once you know that you can develop your skills with practice, determination, and (this one is optional) an annoyingly competitive older brother, it just makes a whole lot more sense to give something a try.

So, whatever you want to be awesome at, this book is here with strategies, hints, and tips to fulfilling your potential and making it happen.

MUSIC

SKATEBOARDING

PLUMBING

VLOGGING

SOCCER

List Of DREAMS

PLAYING THE PIANO

ARCHAEOLOGY

DEEP-SEA DIVING

COOKING

WRITING

All you have to do is take one step at a time, beginning by turning the page…

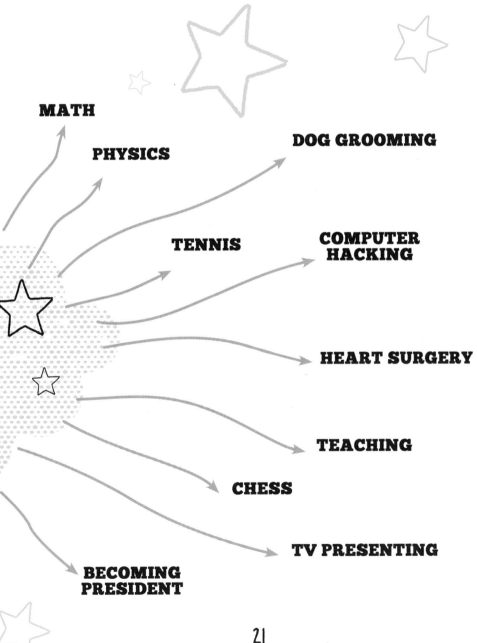

MATH

PHYSICS

DOG GROOMING

TENNIS

COMPUTER
HACKING

HEART SURGERY

TEACHING

CHESS

TV PRESENTING

BECOMING
PRESIDENT

2.

Did you know that two-thirds of kids in school today will end up doing a job that hasn't even been invented yet? That is truly mind-boggling.

And do you know what else? On average, you'll probably have at least seventeen different jobs in your lifetime (but don't worry, you won't have to do them all at the same time).

The world around us is changing so fast. It's no wonder that we sometimes feel **anxious** about how we fit into it. We question whether we are smart enough. We get a bit scared to take a chance in case we look stupid. And sometimes it's tempting to quit before we've even tried having a go at something.

Lots of anxieties and worries can hold us back. So let's take a look and see how we can overcome them. Because it's good to be **READY**. **PREPPED**. **CONFIDENT**. **ON FIRE**! We need to find our confidence to deal with all the changes and challenges that life can bring.

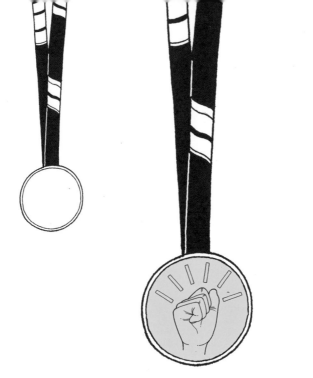

BUT THE CHOICE IS YOURS.

As well as standing on podiums, and having my picture in the newspapers, the journey I went on (and I don't mean the time I got on the wrong bus and ended up in **Bergen, Germany,** rather than **Bergen, Norway**—more on that later) changed me in so many ways. Here are some of the things I learned along the way:

○ No one is born with a table-tennis racket in their hand, a calculator in their head, or Mandarin as their second language.

○ Getting good at something takes time; it doesn't happen overnight. (In fact, especially not overnight—I'm usually asleep.)

○ Becoming **awesome** at something takes time; becoming a world champion takes even longer.

24

Everyone that learns to become good at something has made loads (and I mean LOADS) of mistakes. Here's an example:

"I'VE MISSED MORE THAN NINE THOUSAND SHOTS IN MY CAREER. I'VE LOST ALMOST THREE HUNDRED GAMES. TWENTY-SIX TIMES I'VE BEEN TRUSTED TO TAKE THE GAME-WINNING SHOT AND I MISSED. I'VE FAILED OVER AND OVER AND OVER AGAIN IN MY LIFE...AND THAT'S WHY I SUCCEED."

MICHAEL JORDAN, UBER-SUCCESSFUL FORMER BASKETBALL PLAYER WHO IS NEVER PUT OFF BY FAILURE

MAKES YOU THINK, DOESN'T IT?

○ Anyway, back to our list. No one wants to admit how hard they practice, so don't believe anyone who tells you they are **effortlessly** brilliant or clever. They are probably lying.

○ I don't instantly give up when things get hard. Just because something is difficult doesn't mean that I am terrible and should stop trying. It often just means I haven't found the right strategy (the equivalent of Omega and Mr. Charters) quite yet.

○ I can't be good at everything. I mean, there are definitely a lot of things I could be better at if I actually practiced them. (I tried to mend my skateboard once. I fixed the kingpin but two wheels fell off. DIY skateboard mechanics are NOT recommended.) But there are only twenty-four hours in a day.

Of course, I'm still as likely as the next person to sleepily put my underwear on backward first thing in the morning. I'm **only human**, after all, but I still find it amazing to think that small decisions we make about whether or not to give up on something difficult can have such a big impact on our lives. It would've been very easy in my case to have turned my back on table tennis because I was bad at it. And believe me I was bad! But I didn't. I set my mind to it, persevered, improved my skills, and set off on my **journey** to become the very best I could be.

So, before we look at ways to take on our new challenges, let's look at what might be holding us back. What might make us give up when things get a bit hard? I can tell you from my experience that overcoming these obstacles can only make you stronger.

"NOPE. I'M NO GOOD AT THAT."

The world can be a big, confusing place for sure. But our own minds and bodies are even more confusing. For a start, did you know that there are more life-forms currently living on your skin than there are people on the planet? Supporting that ecosystem is a challenge in itself. And that's before we've even begun to try and find our place in the world of **social media**, exams, and friendship groups.

So starting something new or trying something hard can seem like a whole pile of extra effort. We've all been there. When faced with something tricky, it's just so easy to go "nah" in order to avoid giving it a shot and risk the shame of failing badly. But you're never going to fulfill your potential if you're too scared to even try. So, to understand why we do this, let's take a closer look inside the human brain.

Imagine if you could actually do that? Imagine if you could really look inside the slimy, **jellylike** mind of your friends (I dread to think what you'd see there…).

Physically, the human brain is extremely fragile. It weighs the same as a large cantaloupe melon and has the texture of squishy minced beef (I'm thinking you might not want spaghetti bolognese or melon for dinner after this…). But from an emotional perspective our brains can be pretty fragile, too—and sometimes it's our thoughts and worries that can **sabotage** us and hold us back.

So what runs through your mind when you think about trying something new, something you know might push you out of your **comfort zone** and be "a bit hard"?

27

1 FEAR OF LOOKING FOOLISH

A good friend of mine used to tell me that she wanted to be famous. She wanted to be in films. *Star Wars* in particular. I didn't think that was a bad idea. She was dangerously capable with a toy lightsaber, so I was pretty sure that if the part of Princess Leia's sister ever came up, she'd get it.

But she knew that breaking into a major Hollywood movie from her bungalow in Reading wasn't going to be easy. So she decided to start the process with a part in the school Christmas nativity.

I admired her. I was too **nervous** even to go to the audition. So I didn't and ended up in the audience instead. And I was quite jealous when her name appeared in the program on the big opening night…

EMMA SMITH —2ND CAMEL

It was all set to be a great night. Her dad had borrowed the costume from a friend at work (two humps, since you ask), and her parents, my parents, and I sat together in the front row. Emma was playing Second Camel. She had five lines. Two of them had to be sung. There were four camels in total. **Camel 1** was the main camel. She had eight lines. **Camel 3** and **Camel 4** didn't have any lines. I wasn't really sure what the point of them was, to be honest.

Halfway through the show, the moment arrived. The music built, **Camel 1** sang her lines at perfect pitch, and then it was Emma's turn. But she looked at me just as she was about to open her mouth and I could tell that something was seriously wrong. I could see the terror in her eyes and I just knew she couldn't remember the words. Like a maniac, I started furiously mouthing them back at her. I was **word-perfect** because we'd been practicing in between breaks at Omega for the last three months.

But the lights were dazzling in her eyes, and so she couldn't see my frantic offer of help. So she froze. Standing completely still in front of two hundred people, three other camels, Joseph and Mary… the works. The music teacher played the tune again, to give her another chance. But Emma had lost her nerve. She was overcome with fear.

Camel 1 came to her rescue and belted out the lines and then the song moved on. Most of the audience hardly noticed. But Emma was so upset. The dream of Hollywood stardom was looking a lot less likely now. And at the end of the scene, she raced off the stage so fast she crashed into the lighting tower and crushed her second hump. Her dad was not popular at work when he had to give the costume back. All in all, it wasn't a great night for her.

Emma really took it to heart. She felt like a fool. A failure. "Who can't even remember two lines?" she asked me over and over again. It was a whole month before she could even bring herself to look **Camel 1** in the eye. **Camel 4** couldn't stop himself from telling her that he would have done a much better job.

But she was determined that wouldn't be the end of it. The following year, the school production was Joseph and the Amazing Technicolor Dreamcoat, so Emma put her fears to one side and went to the audition. She wanted **the big part**, the one with the fancy coat, but annoyingly **Camel 4** got that. She got back out there, though, and faced her fears. And this time, she nailed it.

I suspect that on some level everyone can relate to this story. Putting yourself out there, **taking a risk** in front of others, is a scary business. Have you ever decided not to put your hand up in case your question is a stupid one? Or perhaps everyone has always told you that you're a super-talented runner. But this year, you're on the start line for the 100m sprint, and the opposition seems a little tough. Like they've been training with Usain Bolt. You'd rather not break your winning streak, so you decide to stage a stomachache. This has to be better than the humiliation of coming last, surely? Much better to blend in with everyone else than to risk people laughing. It is entirely natural to want to fit in.

So, the moral of this is, never borrow a camel costume. And…

BE BRAVE!

You don't get good at stuff if you are so worried about looking foolish that you don't go to the audition, or you never ask a question. You don't improve if you pull out of the race when you see the competition. You'll never learn anything new that way.

2 EVERYONE IS WAY BETTER THAN ME.

Everyone loves a success story. When people win talent shows on television, we rate them for the skill they've shown onstage. Whether they're singing, dancing, or making things vanish into thin air, we see a faultless performance… and refuse to believe that we could ever do the same thing.

Why is this? What is it about everyone from star athletes to pop stars that makes us think we couldn't hope to be anything like them? The answer is very simple, because the fact is when we see them perform, we're only looking at the end result of a huge amount of hard work. We're watching them with "**success goggles**" on. Whether it's learning the violin, swimming, schoolwork, or BMXing, we don't see how much time and dedication they've put into becoming really good at it. Nor do we see all the mistakes they've made along the way. Instead, we focus on the finished product, assume it must be down to some natural-born talent or gift, and write off our chances of following in their footsteps without even trying.

What's more, when people achieve something big, they tend to bask in the glory of the moment. Often, they're reluctant to admit just **HOW MUCH** work they have put into getting there. It can take away from the fairy-tale ending, after all, but sadly it masks the reality: that amazing feats of awesomeness take hours of practice to perfect.

3 HARD WORK IS FOR OTHER PEOPLE.

When it comes to being lazy, young people can get a bad rap. You can't sleep in for more than half an hour without someone making jokes about whether you're going to get up in time for dinner. But, at the same time, it's fair to say that the most attractive path for some is often the one that requires the least amount of effort. There is another danger out there, though. A great white shark in the water. What happens when everyone around you is telling you "**you're a genius at math**" or "**you've got reaction speeds at the outer limits of human possibility**"? (Someone actually wrote this about me once—I had it above my bed for about six years!) Can you see the problem? You start believing the hype! You begin drafting your Oscar acceptance speech! You plan your post-exam celebrations! All before you've actually made the grade or arrived on the winners' podium.

When people think they are already super talented, they can sometimes get a bit lazy. "Hard work is for people without my genius," they might think. So they take their foot off the gas, stop trying as hard. And end up being overtaken by those who didn't opt for the sofa after their first taste of success.

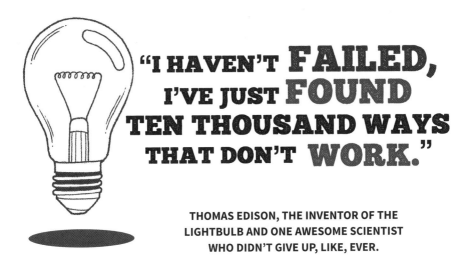

"I HAVEN'T **FAILED**, I'VE JUST **FOUND** TEN THOUSAND WAYS THAT DON'T **WORK**."

THOMAS EDISON, THE INVENTOR OF THE LIGHTBULB AND ONE AWESOME SCIENTIST WHO DIDN'T GIVE UP, LIKE, EVER.

It's tempting to see successful people through your own "success goggles," but let's smash them into oblivion by looking at a...

FAMOUS FAILURE

STEVE JOBS

TECH VISIONARY? ✓

FOUNDER OF APPLE? ✓

FAILURE? REALLY? ✓

Yep. Really. Steve Jobs has gone down in history as the man who gifted the world the iPhone, the iPad, and the iMac. If it's on your Christmas list, and it has an apple on it, chances are it's down to the genius of Mr. Jobs.

HE DOESN'T SOUND LIKE MUCH OF A FLOP...

Well. Even though Steve Jobs founded Apple, after nine years building up the company, he was forced to leave after a disagreement with the people he had brought in to help run it. Ouch. Imagine having to say goodbye to nine whole years of hard work, not to mention seeing other people take over YOUR company. It would've been only too easy for Steve to quit the tech world altogether. But he didn't.

Instead he focused all his energy on other projects, including Pixar—the animation company that went on to produce *Monsters, Inc.*, *Cars*, and *Finding Nemo*. So far, so awesome. But there was more. He also founded a new tech company called NeXT, which, after ten years, was bought by… Apple! And twelve years after he had left, Steve Jobs became the boss of Apple once more!

"I'M **CONVINCED** THAT **ABOUT HALF** OF WHAT SEPARATES **SUCCESSFUL ENTREPRENEURS** FROM THE **NON-SUCCESSFUL** ONES IS **PURE PERSEVERANCE.**"

STEVE JOBS

4 CONFIDENCE CRISES

I used to be pretty low in the confidence department. Sometimes my mom and dad would have their friends over at our house. And before the boring adult chat had started, my dad would make a point of getting my brother and me to introduce ourselves.

All he wanted was a "**Hi, I'm Matthew**" from me. Pretty simple, he thought—and you can't really blame him. But I used to quake at the thought of it. The whole idea of having to speak in front of other people, to someone I hardly knew, made me want to hide under the nearest duvet for a week.

But something changed.

And now, these days, people ask me to give speeches. Maybe to a whole school or a business. I suspect they ask me because I am much cheaper and easier to get hold of than Serena Williams, but (so they tell me) they also want to hear my ideas about how to get good at stuff.

After I give my speeches (sometimes to hundreds of people), it is often the case that someone in the audience comes up and tells me that I am brilliant at **public speaking**. And (almost always) that they are "hopeless" at it. They talk as if I were actually born onstage, my first words being "Ladies and Gentlemen" rather than the usual babbles of ordinary babies.

If only they had seen me at fourteen years old.

Unable to say

"HI, I'M MATTHEW"

to my parents' friends Mandy and Tim, who had popped in for a sherry at Christmas.

So what changed?

I'm going to tell you a secret. I practiced for years on how to speak confidently in public. I went to a debate club called Toastmasters. They don't teach you how to make really tasty bread-based snacks (although that would also be a winner), no, they are the Omega club for public speaking rather than table tennis. And at this debate club, you have to **get up and speak** about topics you might not be familiar with. In front of actual people you've never met before.

It is pretty scary the first time you go. But the more you do it, the more they help you, and the more you watch other people in the same situation (terrified) as you—the easier it becomes.

Once I'd delivered some awful speeches at the debate club, I knew how to handle it. I knew how to make the next speech just that bit better. I wasn't afraid of a room full of people I didn't know. I wasn't worried they'd laugh, and I knew what to do if they did.

Practice built my confidence. I wasn't born with it.

5 WHO EVEN AM I?

In some ways, life would be so much easier if we all shared the same outlook as our friends. If we all had the same fears and ambitions, then there'd be no chance of having a go at something different and failing. But how dull would that be? The fact is that every single one of us is unique. We look different (apart from the time I thought it was a great idea to buy the same Shrek-green—yes, green—cardigan that my best friend had). We think and behave like nobody else, and we all have the potential for **awesomeness**.

But doing our own thing and dealing with the attention that brings takes confidence, which ultimately has to come from feeling

HAPPY
IN OUR
OWN SKIN.

When we consider everything that can hold us back, it's a miracle that we get out of bed in the morning. Then again, every second of each day someone in the world pushes themselves out of their comfort zone to achieve great things.

Somehow, *they've* looked inside their brains and found a way to tackle all the doubts, insecurities, and temptations that might have otherwise stopped them from pursuing their **ambitions**. And if they can, then you can too.

So, how do we make sure the things that hold us back, well, don't?

MISSION IMPOSSIBLE? NOPE!

YOUR MISSION IS TO THINK ABOUT MINDSET.

Our **mindset** can be described as the way we look at the world and our place in it. And it turns out that this mindset (if we don't get it right) can seriously hold us back.

Carol Dweck is a psychologist who has done oodles of research into the mindsets of young people. Her work is amazing (she's a professor who studies everything about mindset) and she has shown that it really can either hold you back or help you get good at stuff. She's tested it. She has "experimented" on actual people (don't worry, no one was harmed in the process) to look at what holds us back or sets us free to pursue our ambitions. It is science. And there is lots of research and evidence to back it up.

And guess what Professor Dweck has found? There are two types of mindset: one is pretty fantastic in helping us to become good at stuff; the other not so much.

OK, so let's start with the problem one. The **FIXED** Mindset. This is where people think that you can **only** be good at something if you are born "gifted" or "talented." That you pop into the world already hardwired to be:

GOOD AT MATH,

BRILLIANT AT TENNIS,

ABLE TO
SING LIKE AN
OPERA DIVA,

OR
NAIL THE
DRAGON FLIP
ON A SKATEBOARD ON THE FIRST GO.

In a Fixed Mindset, you believe you've either got a talent for something or (more disappointingly) that you haven't. And there is not very much you can do to change that, no matter how hard you might try. But can you see the problem? If you believe that people are either born great at things or they're not, then where does that leave practice or trying hard to improve? Right at the bottom of a totally pointless list of totally **pointless things**. You just wouldn't bother. It wouldn't be worth the effort. You'd be better off spending your time digging a hole to Australia in your back garden. Which I did with my brother once. We got quite far (about seven feet). We even convinced the local vicar to help us (not quite sure how, he really must have had better things to do). Any way you look at it, it was a pretty pointless exercise.

Remember **Kid Average?** He was in a Fixed Mindset. He didn't see the point of trying to improve his table-tennis skills and just walked away. **Kid Awesome** stuck at it. He wasn't born with a table-tennis racket in his hand. He just believed that he could improve. Just **thinking** that meant it was worth a shot. He wasn't in a Fixed Mindset, and over time he changed his ability from average to awesome with practice, the table in the garage, and that competitive brother available 24-7.

Now this is a problem because Professor Carol Dweck thinks that more than **40 percent** of us might be in a Fixed Mindset.

That's a lot of people. In fact, that means there could be as many as 2,960,000,000 people in the world with a Fixed Mindset. That's more than the population of Europe and North America combined. Wow. You can see the issue.

THIS IS MASSIVE.

TOP TEN FIXED MINDSET THOUGHTS

It's normal to doubt your abilities sometimes, but your thoughts can become a pattern that can hold you back. Do any of these phrases sound familiar?

WE'RE ALL HOPELESS AT MATH IN OUR FAMILY.

I'M NOT REALLY GOOD AT ANYTHING.

My memory's terrible; my French vocab just won't stick.

I often START things but never FINISH them.

I'd rather DIE than stand up and SPEAK in front of people.

I DON'T HAVE THE COORDINATION FOR TENNIS.

EVERYONE is way better than me at science—I just don't get it.

DRAWING! You're kidding, I can't even draw a stick figure!

My sister's the CLEVER ONE in our family.

Hard work is for other people. I'm a natural.

I'll hazard a guess that you've heard lots of these before. You might have even have said some of them yourself. Fixed Mindsets are everywhere, and they hold people back every single day, so why not try to ditch them from your language right now?

HOW FIXED MINDSETS HAPPEN

As we found out earlier, Fixed Mindsets are super-common, but did you realize that people can fall into them when they are really quite young? A friend of mine told me a story the other day about why she had always thought she wasn't very clever. When she was in elementary school, there were two groups for reading: the Rockets and the Turtles. She was a Turtle. Can you see the association? Rockets zoom and turtles plod along slowly. You get the picture. The Turtle group was not seen as "talented" at reading. And as a consequence, the Turtles didn't really try. My friend has thought of herself as a Turtle, rather than a Rocket, for almost forty years (which is actually pretty young in turtle years, but that is not the point I am making).

It's possible that small things people say or do can drive us into a Fixed Mindset. And we can end up being Turtles rather than Rockets forever if we are not careful. Not practicing. Not improving.

But people who *do* try and who *do* get good at stuff are in what's called a **GROWTH Mindset**. Top soccer players, Oscar-winning actors, the best in the class at math. Anyone who is any good at anything is probably in a Growth Mindset. A Growth Mindset is one of the biggest secrets to success.

SAY HELLO TO THE GROWTH MINDSET.

CHECK YOUR MINDSET

Here are some common attitudes that can help you figure out if you are in a GROWTH or FIXED Mindset. You may not sit easily in one mindset or the other, or you might be in a Growth Mindset about some things and a Fixed Mindset about others.

GROWTH MINDSET

ABILITY
Ability can be changed with practice. Talents, gifts, and skills can be developed.

EFFORT
It makes sense to have a go at anything. Putting effort in is the only way to get better at stuff.

MISTAKES
Mistakes happen. They are nothing to be ashamed of and they show me exactly what I don't know so that I can work on improving my skills.

FEEDBACK
I appreciate feedback. Unless I know where I'm going wrong, I'll never be able to improve!

FIXED MINDSET

ABILITY
Ability is fixed and predetermined from birth. People are born with certain gifts, talents, or skills.

EFFORT
What's the point in trying? My abilities were given to me at birth and I can't change them.

MISTAKES
Let's not admit we make them. Let's carry on exactly as before. And let's definitely not ask anyone for help. Super-talented people don't need help!

FEEDBACK
I don't need it. It makes me uncomfortable, so I usually just ignore it.

But thinking about your mindset will bring you one step closer to better understanding your personality and how to achieve your awesomeness. Which of these sounds most like you?

CHALLENGES

I welcome a challenge. Bring it on! Trying new things is the only way to learn. I don't mind if I don't get it right the first time. That's fine. I'll get it next time, or the time after that…

OTHER PEOPLE'S SUCCESSES

I always try to find out how others achieved their goals. What did they do? How can I do the same as them to achieve success?

RESULT
KID AWESOME

Look out world, I'm coming! And I'm going to work as hard as I can to be the best me I can be!

CHALLENGES

I don't like challenges and usually avoid them at all costs. I don't want to look stupid, so what happens if I try something and get it wrong? What if I lose? I'm better off just not partaking at all.

OTHER PEOPLE'S SUCCESSES

I get jealous of other people's achievements. And I also get a bit defensive as I assume I'm not as good as them.

RESULT
KID AVERAGE

Maybe I'll dig a hole to Australia from suburban Reading for the rest of my life.

WHAT IS A GROWTH MINDSET? AND CAN I BUY ONE ONLINE?

The bad news is you can't order a Growth Mindset online to be delivered with an order of garlic bread on the side. The good news is you can **train yourself** to have one.

A Growth Mindset is the belief that your ability is not fixed. You are not handed out a fixed pot of brilliance at birth (that might only be half-full in some cases). Instead you can grow and change your ability with practice. With **determination**. With **effort**.

Once you believe that opportunity (remember that table in my garage?) and dedicated practice (remember I wanted to smash my brother?) are the foundations of getting good, well, then it makes sense to have a go. After all, these are things you can control.

FIXED MINDSET VS GROWTH MINDSET

If you're in a **FIXED** Mindset, but keen to be in a **GROWTH** Mindset, check out how to overcome some common doubts that might otherwise hold you back.

"**GROWTH MINDSET** is based on the belief that your basic qualities are things you can cultivate through your efforts."

PROFESSOR CAROL DWECK

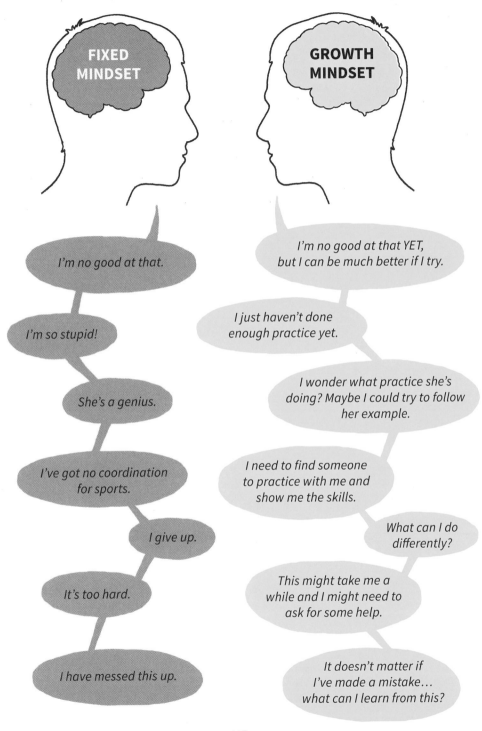

LET'S GET A BIT REAL
(BUT ONLY A TINY BIT).

Growth Mindset is a big deal. Massive. Potentially world-changing. Will it stop global warming? Could it cure cancer? (Well yes, it might if the scientists working on global warming or cancer are in a Growth Mindset and don't give up until they find a solution!)

What we do know for sure, though, is that you definitely won't reach your potential if you don't even try. And even if you are not the Olympic champion at the end of all this (I wasn't; it turns out most of the population of China also had a table-tennis table in their garage and hadn't wasted quite as much time as I had on the hole to Australia), you'll be far, far better than when you started. The best you could possibly be.

You'll probably be more **confident**, more willing to try new things, and less frightened of looking stupid.

So I think we're ready. No, not for the story about the bus to **Bergen, Germany**, not **Bergen**, **Norway** (they are 788 miles apart according to Google and Interpol, who had to come looking for me, but more on this later).

I think we're ready for the next phase of our "awesome" mission: Stage 2.

Let's get on with it. How do we actually get a Growth Mindset and change those Fixed Mindset voices we hear in our heads…?

OVER TO YOU:
· · · · · · · · · · · · · · · · · · · ·
THE WORRY JAR

What are the things you tend to worry about that might stop you from trying something new or hard? Can you write them down on some slips of paper?

Then put the slips in a worry jar—any jam jar or pot will do. In a week's time (or even two weeks) look at the slips of paper again (maybe together with your mom or dad or friend) and see whether those worries still apply. Throw away any that don't.

Then take a look at the ones that are still worrying you. Is there someone you can talk to about these?

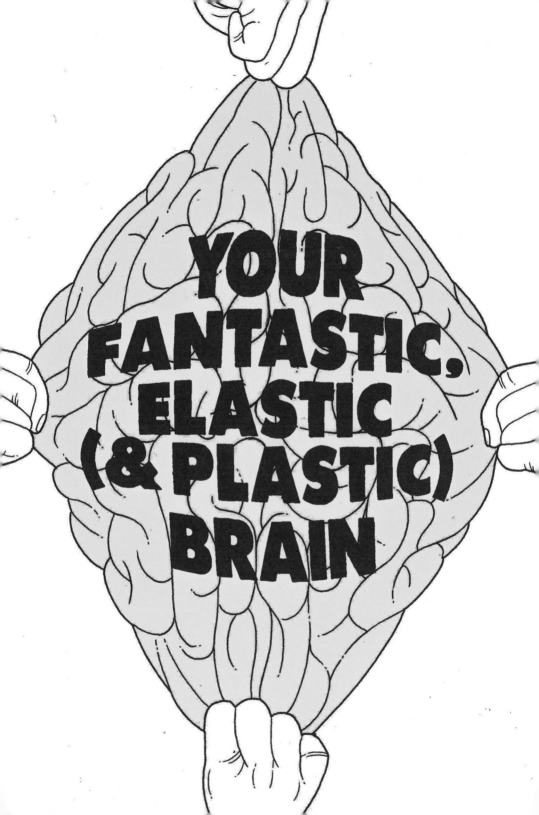

3.

Some weird facts about your brain: (one weird fact is that I can't ever actually type the word "brain" without making a mistake. I type "Brian" and have to correct it. Every. Single. Time. And who is Brian anyway?)

BUT BACK TO THE POINT...

○ Your brain is more than 70 percent water. Being dehydrated affects your concentration and memory (quick, get some water!).

○ Your brain has about **one hundred billion** neurons.

○ There are around one hundred thousand miles of blood vessels in the brain. If you untangled them all, they'd stretch nearly halfway to the Moon.

○ The average person has about sixty thousand thoughts every day.

○ Your brain produces enough electricity to power a small lightbulb.

○ **Sphenopalatine ganglioneuralgia** is the scientific term for brain freeze. Try saying that with an ice-cream headache!

But these facts are not even the most interesting things about the brain. There is something even more amazing, staggering, and, dare I say it, **world changing**. This is relatively recent news even for the neuroscientists out there (perhaps one of them is named Brian?) so we really are at the cutting edge of science here.

The fact is, you can actually **train your brain**. Sort of take it to the gym, if you like. Make it stronger, and grow its capacity for learning new things.

Getting in shape usually means one thing, right? Physical fitness. The body really is an incredible thing. We can train it to be super-flexible or built for endurance sports, like marathons. Physically, our bodies are fully adaptable.

But it's also possible to **customize** your brain and get it in good shape—and fortunately, that doesn't involve spending hours in the gym…

YOUR MARVELOUS ~~BRIAN~~ BRAIN

Day after day, our brains are hard at work. They are Mission Control for every move we make, from blinking and breathing to walking and talking. Your brain might power down a bit at night, but even in sleep mode it is processing information and making sense of it.

REVISE

BREATHE

RUN

But the brain is also a complex communication center. It's made up of billions of pathways that deliver signals to our central nervous system, which controls all activities in the body. These are called neural signals. Their job is to fire up every time we think, feel, or do something. Some pathways are more active with signals than others. There are pathways in charge of basic functions that keep us alive, of course, but lots more are formed because we choose to DO certain things. From playing the guitar to learning lines for a school play, neural pathways take shape to deliver the signals we need to get that particular job done.

PLAY GUITAR

SLEEP

This means we can shape up our brain just like we can shape up our body. Think of it as a mental muscle. If we put the brain through a fitness program that helps to build neural pathways, we can mold it into something truly incredible. And the more we push ourselves, the more connections we make and the stronger they become. Scientists have a name for this. Wait for it—it's called…

EAT

NEURO-PLASTICITY.

SKATE

GET CONNECTED.

As well as being a table-tennis player, I'm a writer and **journalist**. I've been doing it for a long time. When I started writing, my table-tennis pathways were still very active. My chop loop shot across the table was pretty awesome. My 1,200-word article on the local soccer game, not so much.

But over time I have developed my writing skills. My brian (darn it! Again!) has adapted. I write better. And faster. I find the best words quicker and put them together more effectively. The more I have practiced writing, the more **connections** I've grown to make me better at it. Sadly, though, my killer spin serve is not what it used to be.

But that's the thing with these pesky little neural connections. You have to use them or you lose them. They're fickle little things. They don't hang around if you're not paying them any attention. The more you practice, the more they grow. If you stop practicing, they're off. Gone. Sayonara. Au revoir. Start-from-scratchville. Think of taking a walk in a forest that no one has ever traveled through before. The first time you try, it will be pretty tricky. You probably won't leave much of a trail behind you, and the plants will grow back quickly in your wake.

But if you keep walking the same route, day in, day out, then eventually you'll create a path. Making it easier to walk through the forest next time. Neural connections are the same. So, the more you **practice** math questions (or skateboarding tricks, or level fifty-three of Minecraft), the stronger the connections become, making it easier the next time you try.

GROW

STRENGTH

"CONTINUOUS EFFORT

—not strength or intelligence—
is the key to unlocking
our potential."

WINSTON CHURCHILL, WARTIME HERO
AND FORMER BRITISH PRIME MINISTER

YOU'RE PROBABLY THINKING, "WHAT ON EARTH DOES ALL THIS HAVE TO DO WITH MINDSET?"

You thought you were getting a Growth Mindset and instead you're now thinking about a **WEIGHT-LIFTING** regime for the jellylike stuff in your skull.

But, surely, this ability for the brain to physically change and create new connections is the very reason that having a Growth Mindset really works. It's proof that your ability isn't fixed at birth. If your brain actually grows when you practice, making things easier to achieve the next time, then it makes a whole lot of sense to start practicing things.

Now your brain isn't actually made from plastic, but it does share the same ability to be molded and shaped. While we can't flatten it out or sculpt it into a model of the Eiffel Tower (just for example), we **CAN** reset the pathways inside it to help us become **awesome** at something we really want to be good at.

If you need proof, then follow me as we jump inside the back of a London taxi and stare at the driver's head. Why? Because something pretty awesome is happening in there…

THE HUMAN GPS

London's black taxicabs are famous all around the world. When you ask to be taken to an address on the other side of the capital, the driver will take the most efficient route there without getting lost or going in the wrong direction up a one-way street. How can they do this without looking at a map or a GPS? Because in order to earn your license to drive a black cab you need to pass an exam called…

THE KNOWLEDGE

A black cab driver is expected to know about twenty-five thousand streets in London, and thousands of landmarks. They also have to be able to drive there from any point in the capital without making a mistake. In the Knowledge exam, taxi drivers are asked to describe the routes they'd take between any places that the examiner might dream up. It's a huge mental undertaking, and requires several years of study before candidates are ready to take the exam. They put in tons of practice, which many hopefuls do by zipping around the streets on a scooter.

Amazingly, brain scans have shown that those who master the massive tangle of roads actually experience structural changes in their brains. They possess more **gray matter**, which is where mental processing takes place, compared to when they first set out on the streets. As they begin to make sense of the way the capital is connected, their brains build up new neural pathways to deal with the information required.

So, if you ever find yourself in a black cab in London, just think that the driver behind the wheel has worked hard at building their…

SUPER BRAIN

Your brain has been specially designed to manage skills involving memory and visual processing. Your cabbie might not look exceptional, but watch them thread through the streets and you'll realize you're in the presence of a human GPS. That's an awesome feat of memory that takes masses of practice. It also goes to show just how adaptable the brain can be when it comes to helping you…

STAND OUT FROM THE CROWD.

TAXI DRIVERS VS BUS DRIVERS: THE MIND MATCH

In a similar piece of research, bus drivers were put under the spotlight with a brain scan.

Now, these men and women have to learn a lot of streets too, but not as many as taxi drivers. And that's the crucial difference. After all, bus drivers follow set routes and don't need to know every single part of the spaghetti bolognese tangle of roads, streets, avenues, and cul-de-sacs that goes into making up London.

So, bus drivers' scans showed their brains had changed too, but here is the interesting bit: their brains hadn't changed as much as the taxi drivers' brains had. Why? Because bus drivers don't need to learn so many street names. The practice isn't quite as challenging, so the bus drivers didn't need to build as many neural pathways in their brains as taxi drivers.

THE MORAL OF THIS STORY IS:

- The more challenging the practice, the more neural connections you build.
- Keep practicing. Don't put down your math homework early if you want to be good at it. If you do, those connections might start disappearing faster than your Uncle Pete's hair. You want your brilliant practice to mean something!

But you don't have to start from scratch. When it comes to shaping your brain to become awesome at stuff, just remember that you've already begun...

OVER TO YOU:

• •

YOUR WORST-CASE SCENARIO

Making everyday tasks harder is a great way of training your brain. Don't be afraid to be curious and try new things, and never let mistakes put you off. Mistakes can actually help to grow your brain!

So… can you think of ways to make your skate practice or your math homework or your dance rehearsal just that little bit trickier, to push you further?

4.

Now here's an interesting thing. As human beings, we are becoming better at stuff all the time.

In every area of endeavor, from sports to science, we are building on experience, raising our standards, and using our brains to drive these achievements. At the 1900 Olympics, the winner of the men's one hundred meters took the title in **eleven seconds**. Today, thanks to the power of practice, that time is regularly beaten by under fifteen's at national school championships. Way back in the **thirteenth century**, an English scholar called Roger Bacon argued that it was impossible to master math in less than forty years. Today, we consider the kind of calculations he was talking about to be basic stuff we learn at school.

So, we humans are better than ever, all thanks to the brain's neuroplasticity, but you still have to practice if you want to be...

And as it turns out, you are already awesome at lots of things.

GETTING GOOD AT STUFF (WITHOUT TRYING)

Let's do a reading test. (Don't groan! Growth Mindsets **love** a test—
they are great practice!)

WHAT DOES THIS SAY?

loweon tetnmis ysea ilhwe a enirwga egelPin otn is nabaan.

AND WHAT DOES THIS SAY?

Peeling a banana is not easy while wearing woolen mittens.

Both strings of letters have the same forty-nine characters. But the
first one is total gobbledygook. Utterly meaningless. The second,
however, makes sense to you. You understand it.

WHY?

Because you have developed a highly complex skill—your pattern
recognition with words in the English language (a.k.a. reading) is
top-notch.

Now imagine a tiny baby. Do you think it would see any difference
between the two strings of letters? No, not at all. Not a chance. None
of us arrive in the world able to recognize the alphabet, so both sets
of letters look like total nonsense to a newborn.

Without realizing it, you've probably spent hundreds of hours practicing reading. It is a hugely complex skill. And I suspect you have never given it much thought. But doesn't it make you think—if you can master this reading business, with practice, why can't you master that violin piece you've been putting off learning? Or nail that science topic that you think is way beyond you? The truth is, there is absolutely no reason why.

Here are some more really complex things that you've practiced loads without really noticing…

1 THE ABILITY TO RECOGNIZE YOUR BEST FRIEND IN A CROWD

Recognizing people we know is a super-tricky thing to do. Think about it. Almost everyone has the exact same features. Two eyes, two ears, and a nose. But tiny differences in appearance become really obvious when you've spent a lot of time looking at other people. With all the practice we've had, we've unconsciously become really good at facial recognition.

Imagine you're trying to pick out a particular rat from a lineup of forty rats. Not a chance you'd pick the same rat out twice, right? But put forty kids in a row and you'll pick out your best friend every single time (let's face it, it'd be friendship-ending if you didn't).

2 ROCK, PAPER, SCISSORS

Everyone knows that this is the best way to decide anything. Not sure why politicians don't use it more often. I actually won my brother's new bike off him after I convinced him to go to a best of three. That's the thing with rock, paper, scissors. NEVER go to a best of three if you won the first go. Ever. Quit while you are ahead. He didn't give me the bike. He was very angry.

But let's get back to the point. Rock, paper, scissors is a very complex thought process for our brains because of the mental backflips we do when trying to anticipate our opponent's next move. The more you play it, the more your brain becomes fine-tuned to the movements of the other person. You know, like that wild hand movement your mom makes when she's decided to go scissors. And then, if you can convince someone to go to best of three, you actually start weighing up probabilities in your head. Is your dad really going to go rock three times in a row?

So, who said you can't do math?

3 RECOGNIZING PATTERNS

Why do we look both ways before crossing the road? How do you know to run into the space on the soccer field where your friend can pass to you unmarked? Because you've seen these patterns before. You have learned to assess the risks, the benefits of staying put for a few extra seconds, the likelihood that he'll kick the ball properly for once, and not hoof it off the field like an over-enthusiastic horse.

WARNING: Sometimes our pattern recognition is a bit too good, though. That's why people sometimes think they see the face of Jesus in a piece of burnt toast. Or look at a cloud and think it looks exactly like Taylor Swift's latest haircut.

So, we're already brilliant at loads of complex things. We are, in all honesty, already totally awesome. You just need to apply this awesomeness to stuff you'd like to get good at. You've clearly got the skills, now all you need is…

THE PRACTICE.

BUT NOT ALL PRACTICE IS EQUAL.

Not all practice is as useful at growing your brain and creating neural connections. There are different types of practice, and some are much more effective than others.

Yes, I know, this is a bit of a blow. How on earth are we supposed to know what to focus on? Time is precious. We don't want to be wasting it on something that is totally pointless.

So, let's have a look at what this means. Ask yourself this simple question:

CAN YOU RIDE A BIKE?

?

No

Yes

Riding around your friend's back garden is not going to create any new pathways.

Practicing is hard. You're learning a new skill, and adapting your brain.

Can you ride a bike now?

Keep going. You'll get there.

Do you want to be able to do wheelies?

Yes

No

Yes

No

So, try something new.

It's going to be hard. You're going to have to do some tricky practice that is going to train your brain.

Take up stamp collecting. It's less risky.

I hope you've got the picture. The practice that really works, that builds those strong and lasting neural connections, is practice that challenges you. **The Hard Stuff.** The stuff that might make your…

EYES WATER,

MUSCLES ACHE,

and your…

BRAIN HURT.

The screw-your-face-up, grit-your-teeth kind of practice that makes you feel good about yourself afterward because you know you've achieved something.

No one gets good at stuff by practicing the things they can already do. Can you walk? The answer is probably yes. Now that you can do it easily, do you get any better the more you practice walking?

YOU CAN SEE WHERE I'M GOING WITH THIS, CAN'T YOU?

It is all too easy to study for an exam lying on the sofa, one eye on social media, one eye on the page of French words you're supposed to be learning. That isn't hard practice. Getting up, putting your French words away, and reciting them several times to your gran— THAT would be hard practice. You'd make some mistakes, but guess what? You'd also be creating neural pathways in your French vocab learning, and would be more likely to remember the words next time.

Awesome people get good at stuff by doing the type of practice that challenges them. It's a secret to their success. But we're not just talking about people who have become world-famous in their chosen field. Here's how you can practice effectively:

1 SPORTS

Practice with people better than you. And (sad fact) there is always someone better than you (unless of course you are already World Number 1). Practice the hard shots, the tricky passes, use your other foot (assuming it is soccer, obviously; that advice is less useful in swimming: use both feet if you're swimming).

2 PRESENTATIONS TO YOUR CLASS

Recite the presentation in the mirror. Then say it to your cat and then again to your sister. It might be daunting. She (your cat or your sister) might laugh. But it will make it easier when you have to stand up in front of the class.

3 MATH

Go on, do the questions you find difficult, not the ones you can already do. And when you get stuck, don't be afraid to ask for help.

4 LEARNING A LANGUAGE

Speak it. Don't be shy. Speak in public to your friends or teachers who can give you feedback, and tell you where you are making mistakes.

5 PREPARING FOR EXAMS

Don't sit there looking blankly at your notes, convincing yourself that the stuff is going in. Do questions from previous test papers and time yourself to get used to working in test-like conditions.

Remember my brother? The supercompetitive one? The one who still owes me a brand-new BMX? He was older and better than me at table tennis. He gave me the stretching practice I needed in the garage. He was faster than me, stronger than me, better than me. (If you meet him, don't tell him I said that, though. It'll go to his head.)

Later on in my career, I moved all over Europe to get practice partners that were better than me. It was hard—I needed to practice against opponents who could send me shots I couldn't return at first. So I'd be ready (relaxed even!) when those shots came at me in the **Olympics**.

No offense, but I wouldn't have gotten very far playing (for example) your dad for practice. Unless of course your dad is Zhang Jike or Ma Lin, he's probably not Olympic standard, and so not a difficult enough opponent. Practicing with him would be the table-tennis equivalent of walking around my own bedroom.

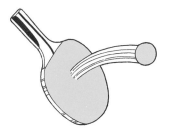

THE SECRET OF PRACTICE

Check out these tales that uncover the "practice secret," and demonstrate how effective practice really **boosts** your performance.

LIONEL MESSI

This international soccer star played a sport called futsal when he was young. **Futsal** is a version of soccer, played five-a-side on a tiny field. It is really hard. You have to be extremely fast and it hones deft ball skills because the field is so small. When it comes to playing on a **full-size** soccer field, the game feels slower. It meant for someone like Messi, who had learned to play an accelerated version of the game, soccer on a full-size field became easier to read and master.

BENJAMIN FRANKLIN

One of the founding fathers of America, a leading politician, an author and scientist. His father told him when he was a child that he was not good enough at writing, so to improve he acquired and read the works of all the great writers of the time. He would then try to reconstruct the entire piece of writing again from **memory**. And then compare what he had written with the original so he could see all of his mistakes. He even translated the articles into rhyme sometimes to improve his language skills!

"ALL HIGHLY COMPETENT PEOPLE, CONTINUALLY SEARCH FOR WAYS TO KEEP LEARNING, GROWING, AND IMPROVING."

BENJAMIN FRANKLIN

GREAT BRITAIN'S WOMEN'S FIELD HOCKEY TEAM

In the run-up to the 2016 Olympics, this team of super-determined women had something called "**Thinking Thursdays**." They still trained hard on all the other days of the week, too, but on Thursdays they really went for it. They were exhausted. At the end of their Thursday session, their coach would ask them to solve problems and think about tactical issues they might face in the next match. Getting used to tackling tricky issues in a state of tiredness made it much easier to think fast when the pressure was on in a grueling match situation.

SIMONE BILES

This American gymnast dedicated her life to training and practice from an early age. She became interested in gymnastics at the age of six and started working with her first trainer at eight years old. By the time she was eighteen, Simone had won so many medals that when she traveled to Rio for the 2016 Olympics, everyone expected her to win gold. And she did—four times over!

Just to reinforce the power of practice and perseverance, here's another…

FAMOUS FAILURE

J. K. ROWLING

The bestselling author, multimillionaire, and philanthropist? The creator of HARRY POTTER? Probably the most successful book series OF ALL TIME? That J. K. Rowling? Right.

Rowling was only thirty-two when the first Harry Potter book was published, and the titles that followed propelled her to stardom. The world she created has inspired films, plays, and even a theme park. And she has gone on to write bestselling novels for adults, too.

SO FAR, I'M NOT SEEING ANY EVIDENCE OF FAILURE.

But. Rowling was unemployed and broke when she wrote her first novel in a coffee shop, with her baby daughter asleep in a stroller next to her. There was no hint of the fame and fortune to come. And even after she had finished the book, twelve publishers rejected her manuscript. Twelve! Turned down Harry Potter! J. K. Rowling didn't give up, though—she believed in her work, even when it seemed that nobody else shared her vision. Her determination finally paid off when an editor saw something magical in the story and gave her a small first offer. And the rest is history!

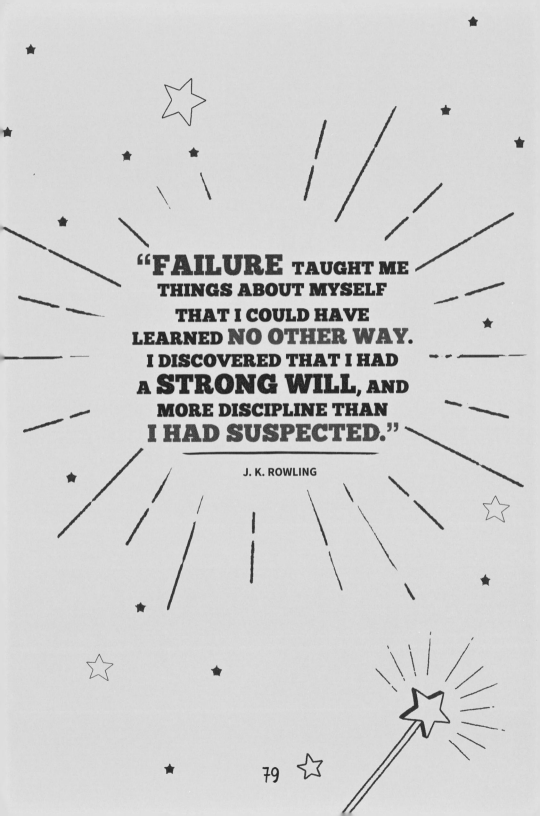

"**FAILURE** TAUGHT ME THINGS ABOUT MYSELF THAT I COULD HAVE LEARNED **NO OTHER WAY.** I DISCOVERED THAT I HAD A **STRONG WILL,** AND MORE DISCIPLINE THAN I HAD SUSPECTED."

J. K. ROWLING

79

MAKE FRIENDS WITH FEEDBACK

When I was thirteen, I had dreams of becoming a spy. So for fun, I used to hide and see how long it would take for my parents to notice I was spying on them. Strangely they never did. At the time, I thought it was because I was Reading's answer to **James Bond**. An awesome spy. Destined for the CIA. Looking back, they probably knew I was behind the TV all along but were so happy I wasn't digging that hole to Australia in their flowerbeds anymore they just let me get on with it.

But, you see. While I thought I was honing my 007 skills, I was actually just sitting in silence on my own. How could I possibly know if I was becoming more like Bond if I never got any feedback?

A bit like practicing basketball in the dark. How would you ever know if you'd got the ball in the basket? You need the lights on, and the knowledge that you missed by a mile or just a millimeter to adapt your attempt next time.

Ice-skaters or gymnasts get almost instant feedback when they try something new like a somersault. How? Because if it goes wrong, they clonk their heads on the floor. It's painful, but a quick way to know that they need to do something different next time. To get really good at something, you need to find your own equivalent of the "**head-clonk**." Preferably someone who will give you honest feedback about where you're going wrong and need to improve. It could be a parent, teacher, coach, or friend—the crucial thing is you trust them to be honest with you. If you're on a **mission** to become good at something on your own, become your own critic. The key is to be honest in your view of how you're doing. It's the surest way to learn and improve.

OVER TO YOU:

. . . .

PRACTICE, PRACTICE, PRACTICE!

Think of something you've always wanted to get better at.

Can you think of three ways you could practice it in a more difficult way to really stretch yourself?

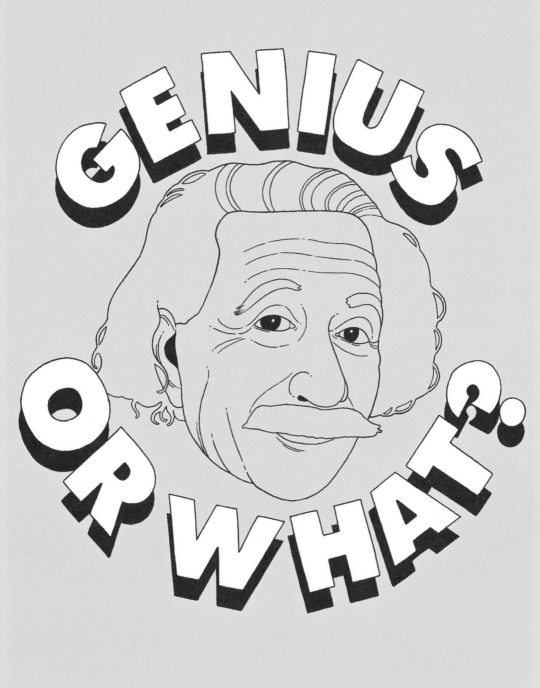

5.

How do you feel when you see...

- An amazing buzzer-beating three-point shot in basketball that wins the game?
- A chess grand master, getting to checkmate in five minutes flat?
- The kid in your class that seems to always do the best on every test?
- The star of the school play, who can remember all of their lines and doesn't seem to get nervous at all?
- The perfect forehand smash in table tennis—taken 50 feet from the table? (Yes, I can. Well, I used to be able to, at least.)

I know. It's tough to imagine Beyoncé as a toddler, or a time when Dwyane Wade had never dribbled a basketball, but these world superstars began life just like you and me. In other words, to get where they are today they had to embrace **opportunity**, try out new skills, and be prepared to get things wrong. Understanding exactly how people become awesome at stuff is crucial to building a **Growth Mindset**.

THE CASE OF KID AWESOME

Remember the table-tennis table in my garage? And the super-competitive brother? When I looked effortlessly good at table tennis at school in my role as **Kid Awesome**, no one knew the full story. And just think about how **Kid Average** reacted when he watched the live coverage of the National Table Tennis Championship Final. As **Kid Awesome** battled for the win, **Kid Average** couldn't believe the level of speed and skill on show. The young contender on screen might've looked strangely familiar to him, but what really commanded his attention was the way **Kid Awesome** dominated the game.

HE'D NEVER SEEN SKILLS LIKE IT!

With his feet up on the sofa, and one eye on the door in case his mom came in and got mad, **Kid Average** watched the winner and no doubt felt strangely flat.

Just then, it must've seemed to him that some people are born to be amazing while others never show a sign of being good at anything. If only he had pressed pause and considered what had **really** gone into **Kid Awesome**'s amazing game.

WHAT KID AVERAGE DIDN'T SEE

One awesome moment. That's what **Kid Average** witnesses when **Kid Awesome** secures his crown as a champion table-tennis player. What he doesn't see is the long, and sometimes difficult, journey that led there. The fact is **Kid Awesome** has devoted hours to challenging practice.

Yes, this moment of victory might have made it all worthwhile, but let me tell you now there were moments in **Kid Awesome**'s journey when he questioned his abilities. Tiredness, defeat, even boredom can become obstacles on the path to awesomeness. It takes a particular kind of determination to overcome them, and even more to use them as a learning experience. Without such challenges and difficulties, in fact, **Kid Awesome**'s final victory would not have been so sweet.

If only **Kid Average** knew that he once stood in exactly the same spot as **Kid Awesome**. There in the garage, before the fork in their lives

NO, NOT THAT KIND OF FORK!

took them in different directions, our ordinary boy had all the same opportunities available to become really good at table tennis and then work hard at becoming the best. Instead, he chose to take the less challenging course through life and walk away from the table-tennis table. As a result, having tuned into the closing stage of the epic journey he *could* have taken, **Kid Average** considers **Kid Awesome's** achievements to be completely beyond his reach.

EVERYONE MAKES MISTAKES!

Nobody hits a perfect note on the first attempt at singing, or finds they can effortlessly dribble a soccer ball straightaway. It's a question of learning from experience and recognizing that any learning experience involves making plenty of mistakes.

When we witness someone performing at a high level, it doesn't make for very good viewing if the pianist we paid to see can't remember the notes, or the racing driver repeatedly stalls the car. As a result, when it comes to success we don't often see the whole story, from the hours that have gone into that amazing performance, to the times they have landed face-first or hit the wrong notes.

When we see someone else's physics exam success, or a great piano performance, or a spectacular win on the tennis court, it is all too easy to fall back into our old ideas of the talent trap. The belief that the person you are watching has been born that way. And presto, **THE FIXED MINDSET** is back!

So let's get into our…

GROWTH MINDSET GROOVE

But first, to help us on our way, let's take a look at another

FAMOUS FAILURE
JAY-Z

As in the millions-of-records-sold, multiple-Grammy-award-winning rapper? The multimillionaire businessman? The man who even managed to marry **ACTUAL** Beyoncé? That Jay-Z?

Not only is Jay-Z one of the most successful musicians of all time, he also owns a record label and has numerous clothing lines, a drinks company, a tech company, and his own music streaming service. And (I really don't think this can be said enough) he married Beyoncé!

IN WHAT PARALLEL UNIVERSE COULD HE POSSIBLY BE CONSIDERED TO HAVE FAILED?

Well. The music business can be tough to crack, as Jay-Z discovered when he first started out. The young hip-hop artist struggled to find a record label that would back him—no one would give him a break. But rather than give up, Jay-Z sold his CDs out of his car, before founding his own record label—and the rest is history. Not only did he create a launchpad for his own music, but he also went on to become one of the world's most successful business visionaries, and responsible for the careers of stars including Rihanna. What a comeback!

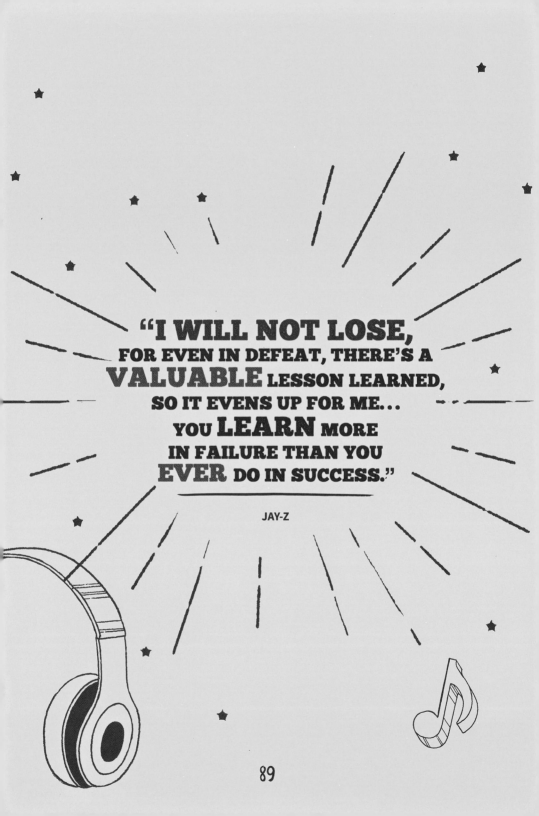

"I WILL NOT LOSE, FOR EVEN IN DEFEAT, THERE'S A VALUABLE LESSON LEARNED, SO IT EVENS UP FOR ME... YOU LEARN MORE IN FAILURE THAN YOU EVER DO IN SUCCESS."

JAY-Z

FINDING YOUR GROWTH MINDSET GROOVE

We know about neuroplasticity. We know it takes a long time to build the neural connections needed to be **brilliant** at anything. So, the performance we are watching must be the result of a lot (really loads) of practice.

No one gets good at soccer by simply stretching before the match. No one aces the physics test just by thinking about Stephen Hawking on the bus to school. These things take time, effort, and determination. They take **PRACTICE**.

And let's face it, this idea of "talent" is everywhere. Roger Federer has been said to have "tennis encoded in his DNA." Simone Biles is described in the US as "a natural daredevil," as if you come into the world all ready to launch into a triple somersault and land straight on your feet. Tiger Woods is said to have been "born to play golf."

So, come with me on a journey to debunk a few famous "talent" myths.

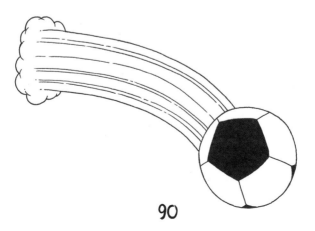

MOZART

WHAT PEOPLE THINK:

He was a child prodigy, composing pieces for the violin and piano by the age of six and producing many works before his tenth birthday. Quite simply, Mozart was born a musical genius.

THE FACTS:

Mozart's father was also a composer and performer, as well as an expert teacher. What's more, he was a dedicated dad, who put his son through intensive musical training from the age of three. By the time Mozart was six, he'd put in about three thousand five hundred hours of practice! Mozart *was* a child prodigy, who composed music when he was super-young, but only because he had done a whole heap of practice under the watchful eye of his dad! How many six year olds do you know who have done all that practice?!

Mozart's masterpiece is Piano Concerto No. 9, which he composed at age twenty-one. Yes, this is still pretty young, but he was no longer a child at this age. And by twenty-one, Mozart had done even more practice. So, rather than being born to play, Mozart actually set out on the road to excellence at a really early age, and worked at it every step of the way.

"I TOO HAD TO WORK HARD, SO AS NOT TO HAVE TO WORK ANY LONGER."

MOZART

SERENA WILLIAMS

WHAT PEOPLE THINK:

A born tennis genius. Super-talented. A sporting legend.

THE FACTS:

Serena started playing tennis with her dad when she was three years old. She played for two hours every day! Seriously, just imagine how good you might have been if you'd played tennis for two hours every single day since you were three. That's not to say that playing so much tennis at such a young age is a good idea. But it **is** to say that so-called child prodigies are not just born with all that skill. They have to work and work at it!

The good news is that Serena loved tennis. It was her passion. She played on courts with potholes and sometimes without nets, which could sometimes make things a bit tricky. Over time, she developed grit, determination, and, most importantly, skill through the thousands of hours of difficult practice she put in. She had an older sister to practice with, to stretch her, too. Serena has also made many mistakes on her journey to sporting-legend status.

Some years after her first Grand Slam win, her world ranking slumped to 139 as she struggled with family troubles and injury. She didn't give up, though. She dug deep, and when she won her twentieth Grand Slam in 2015, she told the crowd (in French, because she'd learned that too) "**When I was a little girl, in California, my father and my mother wanted me to play tennis and now I'm here, with twenty Grand Slam titles.**" Her hard work, determination, and resilience had paid off.

"I REALLY THINK
A CHAMPION IS DEFINED
NOT BY THEIR WINS
BUT BY HOW THEY CAN
RECOVER WHEN THEY
FALL."

SERENA WILLIAMS

THE BRONTË SISTERS

WHAT PEOPLE THINK:

If three sisters can write some of the finest works of English literature, then they must share some special genes.

THE FACTS:

It's fair to say that growing up in rural Yorkshire in the nineteenth century was basically tech-free. With no internet or TV, Charlotte, Emily, and Anne Brontë entertained each other by telling short stories they had made up. They invented entire worlds full of made-up characters, and acted out scenarios between them. They also made friends with feedback—as close-knit siblings, they felt able to criticize each other's efforts constructively, which helped them all to improve.

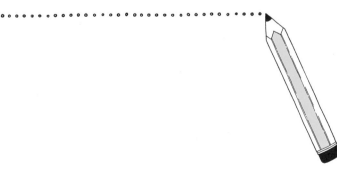

Then the sisters began to write their stories down in tiny matchbox-sized books so that adults couldn't pry and spoil their fun. As time went by, they wrote hundreds of stories, which helped them to harness the power of their imaginations and to practice their writing and storytelling skills—over and over and over again.

One day, when they were grown up, Charlotte found a book of poems written by Emily. Inspired by how good they were, she persuaded her sisters to work together with her on a book of poetry. Again, because they were so close, they were able to criticize and help each other in the most useful way possible. Their poetry book was eventually published, and the women were inspired to keep writing.

Eventually, the sisters went on to pen seminal works of English literature—novels such as *Jane Eyre* (Charlotte) and *Wuthering Heights* (Emily). Classics that are read and loved to this day. And the women have gone down in history as some of the most famous siblings of all time. But their books didn't just happen. The Brontës practiced their writing and honed their craft for years before creating these masterpieces.

DAVID BECKHAM

WHAT PEOPLE THINK:

Beckham scored an astonishing sixty-five goals from free kicks during his career. If you aren't familiar with soccer, just know that sixty-five is an awesome achievement. It led people to say to him, "**It's like you were born taking these free kicks. Soccer must be in your DNA.**"

THE FACTS:

David Beckham (now retired) was an awesome soccer player. He played for England, Manchester United, and Real Madrid, to name but a few teams. He laughed when a journalist suggested that he was born wearing a studded boot. "**No one saw how hard I worked as a kid**," he said. "**No one saw how much I wanted to be good at this**."

How many keepie uppies can you do? I might manage four (at a push, if the ball is bigger than usual). David Beckham could do three when he was seven. So basically the same as you or me.

So what took Beckham from performing a couple of keepie uppies to a number that will blow your mind? Perhaps the best person to answer this is his mom, Sandra.

"**I was amazed at how devoted he was**," she says, remembering how she would watch him through the kitchen window. "**He would start when he got back from school and then continue until his dad got back from work. Then they would go down to the park to practice some more. He was such an amazing kid when it came to his appetite for hard work**."

Slowly, Beckham improved. After six months, he could get up to fifty keepie uppies. Six months after that he was up to two hundred, which I'm sure you'll agree is an impressive number. But by the time he got to the age of nine, he had reached a new record that can only take your breath away: a whopping 2,003!

If you saw someone do thousands of keepie uppies, you would possibly assume they had a natural gift. And you might also think you'd never be able to achieve anything close. Both of these conclusions are completely understandable. What matters is you see through them on your own journey to becoming awesome. It might not make you Beckham, but there's nothing stopping you from becoming so good at something that people just assume you're superhuman, too.

None of this is to say that it is a good idea to focus on one activity from a young age. Often, it is better to try lots of things, and to have fun doing them all, before zoning in on your passion. But it is to say that success is a journey, even for so-called child prodigies. They didn't inherit their success. They just started that journey very early in life!

Appetite FOR HARD WORK

"HUMAN CALCULATORS"

WHAT PEOPLE THINK:

You're either good at math or you're not. Some people have a "brain for numbers." And some can do the most extraordinary calculations in their heads.

While you and I might struggle with 9 x 12, Shakuntala Devi (born in Bangalore in 1929, when TV had barely been invented and no one had even thought of mobile phones) could multiply two thirteen-digit numbers together in her head (so something like 6,984,701,679,175 x 8,354,123,953,691) in twenty-eight seconds flat.

THE FACTS:

When we see a "human calculator," or even someone in class who is much better than we are at math, it is easy to think it must be down to some kind of "talent" or "gift." That the answers appear in their heads as if put there by some "math fairy."

But is there a fairy? Or a set of "in-born gifts?" Or is there a method? Is there a way of practicing this skill? I think there is. Let's have a go. (Don't groan! Where's your Growth Mindset for your math mojo?)

Let's start with 23 x 17. My friend actually got asked this in an interview once. For a job. She got the question right, but didn't get the job. We never understood why.

Can you do it in your head? Possibly. But probably not.

STEP 1: 23 x 10 makes 230. (Let's call this your subtotal—remember this—come on. That's not too tricky!)

STEP 2: 20 x 7? It's 140.

STEP 3: Add 140 to 230 in your head to make 370 (remember this now; this is your new subtotal).

STEP 4: An easy one now: 3 x 7, which makes 21.

STEP 5: Add 370 to 21 to get the final answer—391.

BINGO.

All of a sudden there are five (relatively easy) steps and you've got the answer. The only tricky bit is remembering the process to follow and then at each stage remembering the subtotal to keep adding to.

So, hang on! You have to do some times tables (we know those). And remember one subtotal at a time. That's all?? That's it? Where's the math fairy in all of this?

Suddenly this all seems a lot less tricky, doesn't it? Maybe those "human calculators" don't have superhuman math genes after all. Now, granted, there are more steps involved if you are trying to

multiply 123 x 456, and even more if you're doing 6,984,701,679,175 x 8,354,123,953,691. But the method can be exactly the same. And the method is not that hard, if you want to give it a go.

"IT'S NOT ALWAYS PEOPLE WHO START OUT THE SMARTEST WHO END UP THE SMARTEST."

PROFESSOR CAROL DWECK

CHECKOUT CHALLENGE

A French scientist took two children known as "human calculators" or "math prodigies" and compared their ability to multiply three-digit numbers together (for example, 768 x 376) with a group of checkout cashiers from a French supermarket (Bon Marché). The cashiers had worked at the supermarket for fourteen years and had no "gift" for math other than the practice of calculating the prices of goods they sold each day. This was back in 1826, well before anyone had a calculator, let alone a cash till, and so they did all of the addition in their heads.

The supermarket staff were better, and faster, than the child prodigies. Fourteen years of purposeful practice had honed their math skills.

WHAT TALENT REALLY LOOKS LIKE

Here are the more common words and phrases that a successful individual or team would associate with their achievements:

BELIEF

Open-minded

BEING POSITIVE

PRACTICE!

EFFORT

CONFIDENCE

Making thousands of mistakes

Learning again and again

CHALLENGING YOURSELF

So, the next time you witness a human do something seemingly **out of this world**, imagine yourself in their shoes.

Remind yourself how much work has gone into this moment, and how they started from the same point as everyone else: with a dream and the determination to make it come true.

We are now well underway with our mission to be awesome. We're in a Growth Mindset, our neural connections are growing faster than Justin Bieber's fan club, and we know the best ways to practice.

It does take a while to get good at stuff. There is quite a lot of practice involved. But that's okay, we're up for the challenge, aren't we?

SO LET'S GET TO IT...

OVER TO YOU:

....

GETTING GOOD AT STUFF:

YOUR ESSENTIAL TOOLKIT

So, you've started to shape your **Growth Mindset**. ✓

You're starting to view mistakes not as failures but as learning **opportunities**. ✓ ✓

You're prepared to put in tons of challenging **practice** to improve. ✓ ✓ ✓

° °

YOUR GROWTH MINDSET
MANTRA

Remind yourself of these **key steps** if things start to get a bit tricky.

○ I'm going to **Practice Hard**.

○ I'm going to **Stick to It**.

○ I'm going to **Be Positive about It**.

○ **AND I'M REALLY PROUD OF IT**.

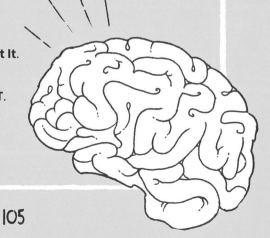

6.

It had been the match of their lives, the 2016 Olympic final! But it wasn't over. The game had ended in a draw and the Great Britain (GB) women's field hockey team were facing a tense penalty shoot-out. They had already pulled off some spectacular play during the match, but the team needed to dig deep for a few more minutes if they were to take home the gold.

The crowd watched. The fans at home held their breath. The players calmly stepped up. **And they did it**. Helen Richardson-Walsh and Hollie Webb scored the decisive penalties that sealed their place in history. The team went wild. The players had given their all, and it had paid off.

BUT IT HADN'T ALWAYS BEEN THIS WAY.

At the Olympics in Athens in 2004, GB didn't even qualify to send a women's field hockey team. In Beijing, they came sixth—there was a long way to go. And people thought Fixed-Mindset things about GB's hockey ability. "**We're not cut out for it**," they'd say. In London in 2012, things were looking up and the team won a bronze medal. But then disaster struck, their coach retired, and the team lost their focus. They came eleventh at the World Cup in 2014—it was a huge setback, and the next Olympics in Rio was only two years away. It was going to be a **mega task** to get the team mojo back, let alone win a medal—and gold was a distant dream.

Something had to be done. So the team made…

They had seen the success the British rugby and cycling teams had had with an idea called **Marginal Gains.**

Marginal Gains sounds quite complicated, but it's actually a super simple and brilliant idea.

Marginal Gains means breaking down a big goal into small parts and then improving each of them, delivering a **huge improvement** in overall performance when you put all the parts back together. So the team got to work. They looked at every single thing that they were going to need to do to win big in Rio. In teeny tiny detail. Let's take a look at just some of what they did…

THEIR FITNESS

They designed a whole new fitness plan. And everyone had to arrive ten minutes before training started. Every day. In the past, the team would turn up right on the dot of the start time (some would be late) and they'd spend time getting ready for the first ten minutes. Taking their headphones off, putting their bags away, filling up their water bottles—you get the picture.

But think about that. Ten minutes a day, five days a week, fifty weeks a year—it adds up to about forty-two hours of lost training **A YEAR**. Wow. That's a whole working week.

Making sure they were 100 percent ready at the beginning of each session gave them…

FORTY-TWO
HOURS OF EXTRA TRAINING TIME. THAT IS A MARGINAL GAIN RIGHT THERE.

THEIR ATTITUDE

To win an Olympic medal, you've got to be in the right mood on the day. You need to be ready. Hyped. Well up for the challenge. **Positively buzzing.**

Being in a bad mood is going to be unhelpful to say the least. So you don't want to be doing anything that is going to make you grumpy. Like sitting on the team bus next to someone who listens to music on the way to the match. How annoying is that—when all you want is dead silence? Or getting changed next to someone who flings their gear around the room like your dad when he can't find his best tennis shorts—when all you want is to be calm and tidy.

SO, THEY CHANGED ALL THAT.

They figured out who liked **silence** on the bus. And they sat together. Always. They figured out who liked to listen to music. And they sat together on the bus too. Always. The calm and tidy changers had one side of the changing room, and the messier ones had the other.

These were small changes. But they created routine and improved everyone's mood before their matches. They were still nervous but they were much more **focused** and much less grumpy. These were

MARGINAL GAINS.

THEIR PRACTICE

We already know that not all practice is equal. And that this team did Thinking Thursdays to practice making tough decisions under pressure.

They also made sure they were practicing in as close to "real" **competition** conditions as they possibly could. They thought about what the weather would be like in Rio in August and practiced for that. They even installed an exact replica of the Rio field at their training ground so the surroundings would be familiar.

Why waste time training on a field that might be a bit different from the one you'll play on in the finals? Surely better to know every inch of the actual field before you even get there?

It's not going to win you the Olympics. But it is going to give you another small advantage. Another

MARGINAL GAIN.

And when these dedicated, determined women added up all their Marginal Gains, the sum was a **MASSIVE** gain in performance…

...it was an
Olympic medal!

THE
GOLD
ONE

Marginal Gains is all about finding and improving the small things that can make a difference. And we can all do this. It doesn't have to be sports; everyone's doing it these days. Businesses are using it to be more efficient and to make more money. Even the Army thinks it's a good idea. So why can't we do it on our **journey to awesomeness**?

Whenever we're faced with a big task, it's natural to feel overwhelmed. Let's say an important test is looming at school. We have to study if we want to do well, but the thought of all that work ahead can make it hard to know where to start.

In this situation, the best advice is to make a study plan. This means setting up a timetable that helps you to cover everything comfortably within the time available. Some areas will need more attention than others, of course, depending on what you're good at and what needs work. With the plan in place, it's much easier to tick off each task in turn, knowing that you'll be ready when you need to perform.

Breaking your workload down into **achievable** chunks is key to a study plan, and Marginal Gains takes a similar approach. So here it is in simple steps:

○ Take a big task.

○ Break it down into smaller parts.

○ Assess each part, and shape up those that you could do better.

○ Put all the small parts back together for a big improvement in performance.

MEET MARGINAL MATTHEW!

I haven't mentioned **The Block** yet. It's such a big deal, I can't quite believe we are only just getting to it now.

When my brother and I weren't in the garage playing table tennis, we were obsessed (and I mean OBSESSED) with **The Block**. What on Earth (you must be thinking) is **The Block**?

The Block is a hardcore, extreme half-mile pavement racecourse around three streets that surround the house where I grew up.

EVERYONE did **The Block** if they came to our house. It was the competition to end all competitions. We timed each attempt and wrote down everyone's results in a notebook that I still have to this day. My mom had a go at it (she walked), while my dad got lost halfway around, which wasn't easy to do. Even the vicar joined in (he was surprisingly fast). You get the picture—everyone had to do it. It was a thing. But it was the competition between me, my brother, and our school friends that was most fun.

THE BLOCK

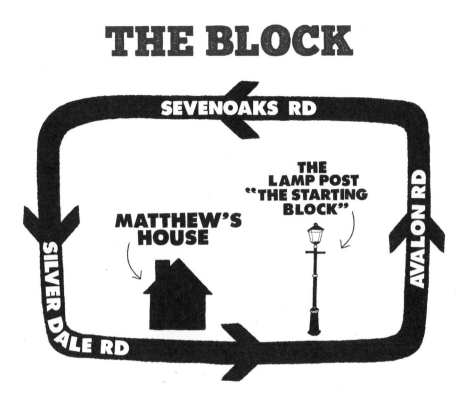

When my brother Andrew broke **The Block's** three-minute barrier, it felt like we'd won gold at the Olympics. We went straight around to Auth's (Mark Autherson's) house to tell him, because he had previously held the record at three minutes, one second. It was an epic day (well, we thought so anyway).

But it didn't stop there. I needed to beat Andrew. He couldn't be top of **The Block**. His name in lights in the results book. No way. Uh-uh.

NOT EVER.

I embarked on a Marginal Gains approach to the situation. I looked at the run, and everything connected to it, and then I broke it down into as many components as I could think of. This was my list (or something close to it. I destroyed the actual list because I didn't want my brother stealing my secrets):

I turned into **MARGINAL MATTHEW.**

I NEEDED to WIN at THE BLOCK aND SO I NEEDED a STRATEGY.

MATTHEW'S MARGINAL GAINS ASSESSMENT

THE GOAL: To go sub-three minutes around **The Block** and do the double by beating my brother.

○ **MY EXERCISE ROUTINE**

I'm busy at school during the week, and I practice table tennis in the evenings. I swim on Wednesdays and run with my dad on Sundays (he needs me to stop him from getting lost).

○ **MY SLEEP PATTERN**

I love reading in bed, and sometimes that means I stay up late. On Fridays, I often have a sleepover at a friend's house.

○ **MY DIET**

I try to eat healthily most of the time, but sometimes I skip breakfast in case I'm late for school!

○ **MY RUNNING GEAR**

My running shoes are brand new. I only have a winter top with long sleeves, which means sometimes I get too hot.

○ **MY PRE-RUN ROUTINE**

I am pretty fit but probably don't do enough stretching to warm up.

○ **MY PREVIOUS RUNS**

I often start too quickly, which can ruin my race. If I get the pace right, I know my finishing sprint is strong.

With all the components laid out in front of me, I was able to look at each one in turn. It made it easier to figure out what was going to help me to achieve the goal of beating my brother. I wrote down what needed to change if I was going to win. I also made a point of highlighting what worked.

- **MY EXERCISE ROUTINE:** I aim to make our Sunday run longer and slower. This will help me to build up stamina.

- **MY SLEEP PATTERN:** I will get an early night on Friday, before the run, and make Saturday nights for sleepovers.

- **MY DIET:** Stop skipping breakfast! It's an important meal.

- **MY RUNNING GEAR:** Save up for a short-sleeved running top.

- **MY PRE-RUN ROUTINE:** No change. Keep it up!

- **MY PREVIOUS RUNS**: Start out steadily and build up the pace toward a strong finish.

So things started to shape up nicely:

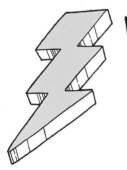

WEEK TIME

WEEK	TIME
1	3 mins, 25 secs
2	3 mins, 27 secs
3	3 mins, 21 secs
4	3 mins, 15 secs
5	3 mins, 12 secs

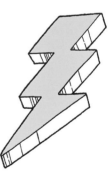

It was looking good. I had set out to fine-tune everything that went into my performance, and I was starting to see an improvement. All those seemingly small details were beginning to add up. The awesome thing was that it started to become even more fun. Andrew was watching my strategy and trying to figure out one of his own, too. So, we were both improving, both pushing each other on. We even started to do **The Block** together, which meant that if one of us was thinking of coasting, the other would have something to say about it. We even did it in the middle of the night once (DO NOT DO THIS by the way. It is dark and there are a lot of hazards). In the end, I broke the three-minute mark, and in the following few weeks, went even faster.

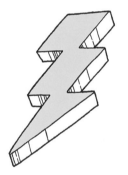

WEEK TIME

WEEK	TIME
6	3 mins, 2 secs
7	2 min, 55 secs
8	2 mins, 49 secs

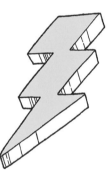

My brother beat his personal best, too, which made me really proud of him (I may not have told him this at the time). We were still battling to be top dog but the competition was making us both better.

By the way, we've still got the results book. My mom and dad still live there. The competition is still open—just in case you want to have a go at **The Block** next time you're in Reading…

MATTHEW'S EXAMS
MARGINAL GAINS **ASSESSMENT**

What's brilliant about Marginal Gains is that it can help to shape up your preparations in every way. Take exams, for example. When studying looms, it's easy to become panicked when you think about how much work you have to cover. A Marginal Gains approach helps you to reduce anxiety by looking at everything that goes into the studying process, breaking it down into smaller components, and then building it back up with confidence.

Let's see how Marginal Matthew (i.e. twelve-year-old me) took his approach to be the best around **The Block** and applied it to his bid to get great grades.

THE GOAL To improve on my exam results from last year

○ **STUDY PLAN**

I need to divide my subjects by the time available. By sticking to the plan, and building in regular breaks, I can cover everything without getting overanxious and tired.

○ **MY DESK**

The table in my bedroom has a wonky leg. It wobbles when I work and makes my handwriting hard to read. Fix the leg (or at least prop it up with a book).

○ **LIGHTING**

Replace the bulb in my desk lamp so I'm not squinting at my books.

EXERCISE

Use at least one break time to run around **The Block**. Not only do I want to beat Andrew, but exercise is a really good way to beat exam stress.

MY PENCILS AND PENS

During my practice exams, I wasted the first few minutes sharpening a blunt pencil and then begging a teacher for a replacement pen as mine had run out of ink. Reclaim those vital minutes by checking my pencil case is properly packed.

PAST PAPERS

Get the exam papers from the previous few years. That way I'll be able to see what the examiners are looking for, and get a feel for the way questions are worded so it will seem familiar when I take the real exam.

HOMEMADE PRACTICE TESTS

This is perhaps the most important thing of all: do a paper in my bedroom under test conditions. Set a timer and get used to working under a time constraint so the real thing doesn't come as a shock. And ask my teacher to grade my paper. After all, feedback is vital if I want to improve.

SHOWER GEL

Make sure Mom doesn't buy that stuff that makes me itch. On the big day, I want to be focusing on my exam and not wriggling uncomfortably like I've sat on an ants' nest.

How far you take Marginal Gains is up to you. The key is to be **smart**, **practical**, and **positive** in your approach. With the changes in place:

- Keep checking how things are going. If you have to experiment or tinker to improve things, that's fine!

- Learn from any mistakes. Failure is the key to improvement.

- Practice, practice and practice again.

- Be patient. Stay cool and focused. The right attitude brings its own rewards.

But what happens if we're pursuing a goal that requires some kind of performance? Whether it's a dance routine or a sporting event, an exam or display, that one final challenge on your journey to becoming awesome might just make or break your success. So, let's look at how to make the experience one of triumph instead of tears…

OVER TO YOU:
GETTING THOSE GAINS

Think about how you can apply this Marginal Gains plan to the things you really want to get good at. It could be:

EXAMS
SKATEBOARD FLIPS
FLUTE PRACTICE
WRITING POETRY
LEARNING A LANGUAGE
A CLASS DEBATE

You name it.

Then make a Marginal Gains plan. Break the challenge down into smaller parts, and work out how you can improve each one.

7.

Disaster struck for me at the Sydney Olympic Games in 2000. It was the last thing I expected to happen. I was standing behind a curtain, waiting to be announced to the crowd for my opening match. My opponent was German player Peter Franz. He shared my ambition and hunger to win, but I had studied his form and felt confident I could beat him.

My preparation had been perfect. I'd spent time at training camps and received advice from a **team of experts** including psychologists and nutritionists. My coach felt sure I could win an Olympic medal, which would've been a dream come true. **I was at the top of my game.** When I stepped through the curtains into the floodlit hall…

THE CROWD TOOK MY BREATH AWAY.

And that was the moment…

EVERYTHING went PEAR SHAPED*

*i.e. very very bad

My opponent, Franz, opened the game. His serve was nothing special. It shouldn't have been difficult for me to return, and yet I struggled. My reflexes, trained to react with lightning speed, felt sluggish. I couldn't understand how Franz could win such an easy point, but things just went…

Even though I wanted this victory badly, **Kid Awesome** had somehow deserted me. I felt like **Kid Average**—way out of my depth on an international stage. In front of a huge audience, I ended up defeated and humiliated. Afterward, my coach told me what had happened in very simple terms:

"Matthew," he said,

CHOKING
(AND HOW TO AVOID IT)

We're not talking about the kind of choke that can happen when you try to stuff down three biscuits before your mom notices.

When it comes to a surprise collapse in performance, at a time when it matters most, "choking" is a term often used to describe the experience. It may not leave you gasping for air, but it's a deeply unpleasant thing for anyone to go through.

○ The first thing to note is that **nervousness is natural**. When faced with a threat, from a sporting opponent to an exam paper, our brain floods our body's system with a naturally occurring hormone called

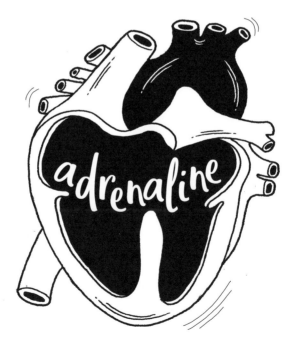

Adrenaline makes our hearts beat faster and our breathing quicken. It is designed to prepare us for one of three physical responses. Either we take on the threat, run away, or get frozen to the spot. We call this a "**fight, flight, freeze response**," and it's designed to help us survive. The trouble is that such a state of

HIGH ALERT
HIGH ALERT
HIGH ALERT

…can also trigger a choke.

1 The key thing in this situation is to realize that this response is completely normal. Everyone gets anxious. It shows we care. It's worth taking a moment to walk around, shake down your arms, and effectively burn off the adrenaline.

2 Focus on your breathing. When your body is fired into a state of alert, it's easy for your brain to trigger a sense of panic. You've gone from being cool and collected to anxious in seconds. Not fun. Breathing is another effective way to help you through this. By focusing on slow, deep breaths in and out, you'll find that sense of calm returning. Why not try the five-seven-nine? No, it's not a bus route, it's a tried-and-tested method for relieving anxiety. Give it a go. Breathe in for five seconds, hold for seven, and breathe out for nine, and so on!

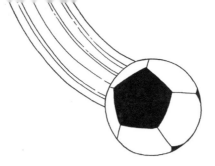

3 Don't overthink it! Let's say you're a top goalie facing a penalty kick. There might be thousands of soccer fans waiting to see if you can make the save. The pressure is on, but before it becomes too much, tell yourself it's just a game like any other. The rules are the same whether you're in a stadium or at the local park with friends. If you can **zone out** of the pressure, and play as you would in the park, you're less likely to think too much about doing something that you've learned to perform automatically—and to perfection.

4 Get things into perspective. So you're about to do something special, from a high-level competition to starting a conversation with someone you secretly fancy. Just then, it can seem like the most important thing in the world. You've been building up to this moment, after all. It's also possible to get so caught up in it that you forget that life will continue no matter what the outcome. It's simply a challenge, and a **learning opportunity** if it doesn't work out as you hoped. It's another great way to manage any pressure you've placed on yourself so you can perform to the best of your abilities.

5 If there is a routine or habit you have that makes you feel less nervous, use it! Loads of people do this. If taking your pet cat for a walk before the exam helps, then do it. If you think you'll remember your lines better with red pants on, that's okay. Coldplay frontman Chris Martin feels he has to brush his teeth before he goes onstage. I used to cut the sleeves off my table-tennis shirts. I thought it helped me win. It didn't. It just made me look like I'd had an accident with a pair of scissors on the way to the tournament.

6 The most important thing to realize is that performing under pressure is a skill. You will get better the more you do it. You will learn to control your nerves, and to embrace them. A **meltdown** isn't a reason to give up, but a chance to learn. As the tennis player Billie Jean King said: "**Pressure is not a problem; it is a privilege**."

Choking can happen to **ANYONE** in a stressful situation—in an exam, on a date, any occasion when you're on public display. You might find that things you can normally do without thinking about them, for example walking, suddenly become impossible. You trip over your own feet, and fall flat. But don't worry, this is totally normal, and happens to almost everyone at some point.

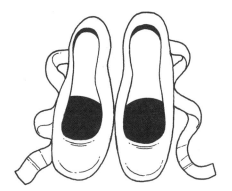

In fact, just to prove **HOW** common it is, here's a…

FAMOUS FAILURE

CHOKING SPECIAL!

JENNIFER LAWRENCE

After winning her Best Actress Oscar in 2013, the actress walked toward the stage to collect her award—and promptly fell down on the steps. While her heavy dress, surprise, and nerves can all take a share of the blame for this, it's fair to say the pressure of the moment also deserves some responsibility!

RORY MCILROY

At the 2011 Masters—a hugely important golfing competition—McIlroy played a dazzling game. Leading the way for the majority of the tournament, he looked set to scoop a great victory. But then—the choke. In the last round, the pressure became too much to bear, and McIlroy's game collapsed. He missed or fumbled so many shots that not only did he lose his lead, he ended up finishing the whole tournament in fifteenth place, instead of first.

OVER TO YOU:
· ·
YOUR WORST-CASE SCENARIO

○ Think about a task or an event that is worrying you, then write down all the things that could go wrong.

○ Now think about what you would do if these things actually happened. For example, if you're acting in a play, then there's a chance that you might forget your lines. In this case, identifying someone you can turn to for a prompt could mean the difference between a minor pause and a major nightmare.

8.

So, as **Kid Awesome** *I'd spent a lot of time in the garage. I was getting pretty good. One of the best in Europe at table tennis. But I needed to stretch myself. Make the practice harder. Mr. Charters arranged for a top coach in* **Bergen, Norway,** *to spend some time with me.*

My mom booked the ticket. She went to the local travel agent (there was no internet back then, and no cell phones) and paid for a twenty-hour coach trip.

I DID THE BLOCK (TWO MINUTES FORTY-NINE SECONDS, SINCE YOU ASK) AND THEN PACKED MY RACKET, SOME THERMALS (IT WAS GOING TO BE REALLY COLD), AND SOME NORWEGIAN KRONER.

I got on the bus. Kicked back. Listened to Michael Jackson on loop (it was the '80s, OK?). Read a bit of *The Lord of The Rings* trilogy and made friends with a few of the German kids in the rows in front. It didn't occur to me until much later that there were an awful lot of Germans going to Norway. And no Norwegians.

After about eighteen hours, we were on the German autobahn. I had a passing thought that Germany wasn't really on the way to Norway but I didn't think too much about it. I was too busy showing Klaus and Jürgen how to do a forehand smash against the bus window.

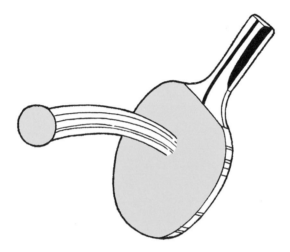

And then the bus began to slow down. Klaus and Jürgen started picking up their bags. High-fiving each other that the journey was over. What? On? Earth? And all of a sudden we're in a lay-by in **Bergen, Germany,** and it dawns on me, my mom bought a ticket…

TO THE  **WRONG** BERGEN.

How many **Bergens** are there? As it turns out, there are two.

I was fifteen. There were no smartphones with GPS (or even the ability to call parents!), no internet, and I didn't have a credit card. The sensible thing might have been to see if the bus driver was going back to Reading anytime soon. But I didn't do that. Instead, I decided to hitchhike to Norway. ★

★ NEVER EVER DO THIS. IT'S DANGEROUS AND **NOT** AT ALL FUN.

Now, on one level, it's a tale about a silly mix-up with tickets, and not paying enough attention, but as it happened to me I like to think it's really a story of grit, determination, and a refusal to give up even when the odds of success were slim…

The POINt of telLING you this STORY?

Well, sometimes life throws you...

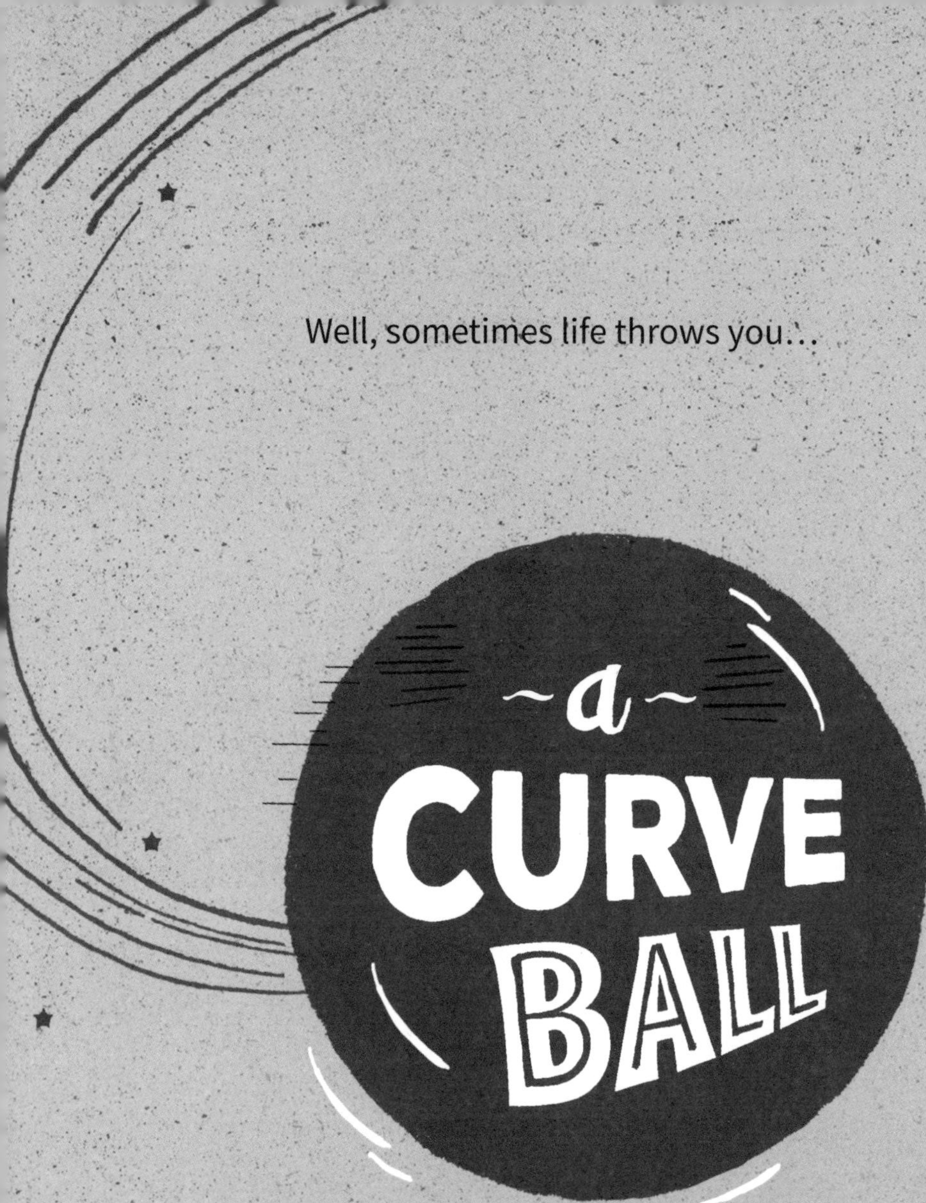

~a~
CURVE
BALL

There can be some real "**What on earth am I going to do now?**" kind of moments. They'll happen to you. They happen to everyone. Probably not in **Bergen, Germany,** and probably not with Klaus and Jürgen. But they'll happen. So be ready. Be set to face anything difficult. And face it with a Growth Mindset (and ideally a fresh pair of underpants).

I made it to Norway. Four days late and with Interpol looking for me after Peter the Norwegian table-tennis coach called my mom to let her know that he'd lost me. I made it via a train station in Denmark where I fell asleep on a bench and someone stole everything I owned. I had no passport, the Norwegian kroner were long gone, as were the thermal vests. And although it was darn cold when I got there, I got there in the end. And the training was **amazing**.

Whatever journey you pick, it doesn't matter how you get there. Just make a start. Grit your teeth if things go wrong. And you'll get there in the end.

It'll be hard but worth it.

"**ANYONE** WHO HAS NEVER MADE A MISTAKE HAS **NEVER TRIED ANYTHING NEW.**"

ALBERT EINSTEIN, MISTAKE MAKER AND AWESOME SCIENTIST

I was an ordinary kid from a suburban town. I started out with little in the talent department. But I practiced hard (and in the right way) and worked for everything with a **drive** and **focus** that I am proud of. I really wanted to be a great table-tennis player. In the end, I won't go down in history. But I got pretty darn good and I really enjoyed it. I traveled the world and met some amazing people along the way.

The same is true of my writing. I was pretty clunky when I started (my editor would say, **VERY** clunky!). But I really wanted to be great at it. I work really hard on it. Even now. Even after twenty years. Every article, every book. I want to make it my best yet. I never give up too easily, and I'm never happy unless I have given it my all.

It doesn't matter if you miss out on being an **Olympic champion**, or a **Nobel prize winner,** or **the president**. It doesn't matter if you get to Norway four days late. It doesn't matter if other people are better than you. What matters is you get out there,

TAKE A RISK,

DARE TO FAIL,

and give it…

YOUR ALL.

Just aim to be the very best that you can be at all times. And I know you'll get there, because…

INDEX

MORE ABOUT MINDSET

BOOKS

ALL ABOUT YOUR BRAIN
by Robert Winston
(DK Children, 2016)

BLAME MY BRAIN: THE AMAZING TEENAGE BRAIN REVEALED
by Nicola Morgan
(Walker Books, 2013)

MISTAKES THAT WORKED
by Charlotte Jones and John O'Brien
(Random House Books for Young Readers, 2016)

MY LIFE, YOUR LIFE: SELF-ESTEEM AND CONFIDENCE
by Honor Head
(Franklin Watts, 2017)

MY LIFE, YOUR LIFE: OVERCOMING FEAR OF FAILURE
by Honor Head
(Franklin Watts, 2017)

ONLINE RESOURCES

A TED-ED TALK ON MINDSETS
https://ed.ted.com/featured/qrZmOV7R

MINDSET EXERCISES AND STRATEGIES
https://www.youcubed.org/resource/student-resources/

**CHALLENGES AND INSPIRATION FROM
THE JAMES DYSON FOUNDATION**
http://www.jamesdysonfoundation.co.uk/students/

**GROWTH MINDSET EXERCISES
YOU CAN DO AT HOME**
https://www.mindsetworks.com/programs/brainology-for-home

**WATCH THE EXPERTS TALK MINDSET AND
THE POWER OF MAKING MISTAKES**
https://vimeo.com/103853269
https://vimeo.com/89521168

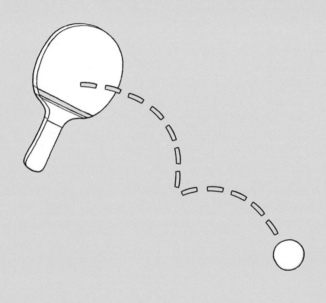